BRICK WALLS OF JUSTICE

Teens Write About
Crime, Punishment, and Alternatives

By Youth Communication

Edited by Laura Longhine

YOUTH
COMMUNICATION
True Stories by Teens

BRICK WALLS OF JUSTICE

EXECUTIVE EDITORS
Keith Hefner and Laura Longhine

CONTRIBUTING EDITORS
Nora McCarthy, Maria Luisa Tucker, Rachel Blustain,
Al Desetta, Marie Glancy, Philip Kay, and Katia Hetter

LAYOUT & DESIGN
Efrain Reyes, Jr. and Jeff Faerber

PRODUCTION
Stephanie Liu

COVER ART
Stephan Vaubel

ISBN 978-1-935552-41-3

Second, Expanded Edition

Printed in the United States of America

Youth Communication ®
New York, New York
www.youthcomm.org

Table of Contents

What's the Charge?

> Max is arrested for no good reason. He spends 24
> hours behind bars and ends up feeling kidnapped by
> prejudiced cops.

Dignity and Respect

> The "Missouri model" of juvenile justice emphasizes
> youth development, rather than harsh punishments—
> and it's been highly successful.

A Day in the Life

> The writer describes life at Riker's Island jail, where he
> spent eight and a half months.

My Little Bouts With the Law

> Mariah shows how foster care, and her search for a
> sense of belonging, led her into trouble with the law.

Life After Prison

> Teens in a youth leadership program describe the
> humiliations of the juvenile justice system and how
> they hope to change their lives.

Contents

My Peers in Prison

> *Outraged by the unfairness of the juvenile justice*
> *system, Olivia embarks on a campaign to educate*
> *people about the system.*

Using the Book

Introduction

Every year, close to a million youth are arrested in the United States. Countless more are stopped by the police. In this book, teens write about their first-hand experiences with cops, crime, and punishment. And they explore what it really takes to help teens build a more positive future.

Gia Minetta and Max Moran write about being unfairly detained by the cops, guilty of little more than being in the wrong place at the wrong time. Unfortunately, their stories are not exceptions, especially for black and Latino youth living in heavily-policed urban neighborhoods. In "What to Do If You're Stopped," Phil Hodge explains how to handle a police confrontation so you don't end up in jail (in short: stay calm and be polite).

Other writers get a much closer look at the criminal justice system. Roger thinks prison will be an easy rite of passage—until he ends up sentenced to seven years on assault charges. He and other writers describe what jail is really like: the humiliation of strip searches, the terrible food and extreme boredom, the anxiety of trying to stay safe, and the longing for home. In "Frontin' for Respect," José carries the reader through a typical day in jail. It starts with him carefully putting on the tough face, posture, and attitude that will protect him from being seen as a target, and ends with a new day that's exactly the same as the one before.

What leads teens into trouble in the first place? Norman B. describes the emotional high of shoplifting, which he starts as a way to be part of the "in" crowd:

"After I'd steal, I'd get this big rush. I'd feel relieved that I'd gotten away with it again. And I'd feel powerful and free."

Stealing also distracts him from the problems he's having at home. He writes, "I felt bad about my life, and the only time I felt a little better was when I was stealing."

Other writers describe finding a similar feeling of release after committing crimes.

In almost every case, prison is not what helps these writers to change their behavior. What helps is starting to see a more positive future for themselves, and experiencing good feelings from succeeding in school and behaving well. To that end, some systems have begun to explore alternatives to juvenile prisons—programs that don't emphasize harsh punishments, but instead, try to help youth make real changes in their lives.

In "Dignity and Respect," "Who Gets a Second Chance?" and "Time for Change," we highlight some of those efforts in Missouri and New York. And in "Get Out and Stay Out," teens offer their best ideas for how juvenile justice systems can make sure that youth who do go to jail don't go back.

In the following stories, some names have been changed: *Busted!* by Gia Minetta.

Ashay Francis

What Prison Is Really Like

By Roger Griffin

My mom died when I was 10 and I went to live in foster care group homes. When I was 17, I moved in with my sister. But times soon got hard and I started selling drugs to help support us.

I was living two lives. In the daytime I went to school and passed all my classes. At night I was in the middle of trouble. I wasn't too worried about being caught, though, because the stories I heard about prison made it seem like nothing.

My mother had told me how bad prison was and described the terrible things that happened there. But the guys on my block made prison seem like a joke. Since they'd been there and my mother hadn't, I believed them.

In the group homes, I kept hearing the same stories about prison: "When I was in such-and-such facility, I was getting visits every day and just chilling doing nothing." Or, "When I was there, I was running the whole jail and doing whatever I wanted."

The kids in my group home would get arrested and come back a couple of days later. They made it seem like it was cool to get arrested. Some people respected them more for being in jail. I figured that the law wasn't serious.

The guys on my block made prison seem like a joke.

So, over time, I became less and less fearful of breaking the law. Not that I wanted to commit crimes, but I didn't believe the consequences would be that serious. After about a year of dealing drugs, I got arrested for possession of a controlled substance. Since it was my first time, the judge sent me home the next day and I lost even more respect for the system. I figured I could get away with anything.

I would soon regret my naïve thinking.

A few months later, my friend and I got robbed by a couple of dudes. Since word got around my whole project, I felt I had to retaliate.

I found out where one of them lived. It was late at night. The street was deserted except for a few people. I got close, he noticed me and started running, and I pulled out a gun. I shot him once in the leg. Then people started looking out their windows and I left.

Two months later I got arrested and was sent to jail, facing attempted murder and assault charges. I was upset with myself, especially when I found out that my girlfriend was pregnant. That made my situation complicated, because I needed to keep my future daughter's well being in mind when deciding whether to take my case to trial.

After six months I pleaded guilty to attempted murder and got sentenced to seven years in prison. I figured I'd be out by the time my daughter turned 5, whereas if I took my case to trial and lost, I might still be locked up when she was a teenager.

When I first got to prison, I was afraid and tense. Nothing looked familiar. The corrections officers (CO's) took our clothes, cut our hair, gave us uniforms, and sent us to our cells.

My so-called friends never told me that that my cell would be 9' x 6'. They never told me I'd be locked up for no less than 18 hours a day, and sometimes for 24 hours. Or that my bed would be as hard as the floor and that I wouldn't have hot water in my cell. Or that the food I'd eat would be unrecognizable, and that I'd take showers only every other day.

I don't recall being told that I would be 10 hours from home and that my girlfriend would have to drive 20 hours in one weekend so I could see my daughter for a couple of hours. I soon found out that recreation meant going to the library or exercising in a fenced-in yard. I had to watch my surroundings because I never knew when a fight or stabbing would happen.

Now, three years later, I sit in my cell and think back on the stories I heard. I laugh at myself for believing them. I wonder, "If I had known the truth about prison, would I be writing this story right now?"

The hardest times are when I'm in my cell all alone. That's when I realize what I did and understand why I'm stuck here.

In prison, the days become repetitious. The only things that change are the names of the prisoners who were beaten up or stabbed, or the guards who were attacked.

I've run into a lot of people who were in group homes with me when we were younger. Sometimes, with nothing better to do, we come up with conspiracy theories on how we got here, only to realize it was our fault. But older men in our neighborhood also helped us get here, because they didn't tell us the truth about prison.

The hardest times are when I'm in my cell all alone. That's when I realize what I did and understand why I'm stuck here. The isolation is the worst punishment. A lot of people go crazy because of it. To avoid thinking constantly about my situation, I listen to music and read all day.

A lot of people in prison believe that they won't be able to become anything positive in life. I don't see it that way. I use my time to plan my future thoroughly, so I can become someone positive once I get out. I will only be in my early 20s when I go home, so I still have the chance to reach my full potential.

I've learned a lot and run into some positive people, mostly lifers who do things like teach black history or run AIDS education and prevention classes.Many of the people who run these classes will never go home, but they try to help those who will. They keep me positive. I respect them because even though they're in a hopeless situation, they don't show it.

It's also helped that my girlfriend moved closer to me, to attend college. Now I can see her and my daughter more often.

My one place of refuge is the prison rec yard, where I leave my suffocating cell and get fresh air. I get a chance to clear my head, contemplate my past moves, and plan the future. I've become a better, more mature, and more responsible person. Looking back, I see that I was irresponsible, immature, and rarely had respect for others.

I plan to go to school when I get out. I hope to find a profession where a felony conviction won't prevent me from getting a job. Sometimes I look back and wonder, "If I went home after school instead of selling drugs, would I have avoided jail? If my family knew I was dealing, would they have stopped me?"

I doubt it. I think I had choose the wrong path to fully understand the consequences. I just hope other young men in my situation don't have to reach that point.

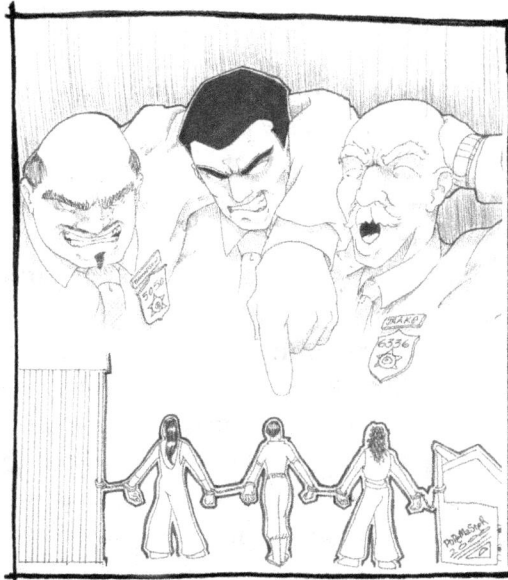

William Pope

Busted!

By Gia Minetta

My friends and I like to hang out together on Saturday night, so it wasn't unusual that a bunch of us were sitting on a stoop one November night around 9:30.

It also wasn't unusual that a police car pulled up and that two cops started walking towards us. You're not allowed to hang out on a stoop unless you live there, and if the cops see more than a couple of people doing it, they'll tell you to move along.

So a couple of us got up and started walking away, trying to decide what to do next. My friend Jane had to go to the bathroom, so we went off in search of a place that would let us use their potty.

When we returned to the street there was still a large group of people on the corner. As Jane and I walked toward them, we noticed that the police car had not left yet either. Then we saw another police car and a police van and hurried to see what was going on.

A couple of officers had a guy backed up against a wall on the other side of the street and were talking to him. I asked people if they knew what was going on, but before I could get an answer I heard screaming and yelling behind me. I turned around to see two cops grab my friend Danny. They twisted his arm behind his back and threw him down face first. When they pulled him up, blood was streaming down his chin.

I flipped. I started screaming, "Let him go! He didn't do anything!" Of course I didn't know if he'd done anything or not, but Danny was like my brother, and the cops were hurting him.

They cuffed Danny and put him in the back of the police van. There must have been 50 of us crowding around and yelling. The cops told us to leave, but no one did. A cop held his club over his head to warn us not to come any closer. Then a female officer told me to back up. When I didn't move, she shoved me. I stumbled backwards and yelled, "Don't touch me, b-tch!"

A cop grabbed my arm from behind, twisted it, and threw me against the police van. Then something hit me hard on the back of the head. I didn't see stars or anything. It just hurt for a while when I touched it. An officer named Cunningham handcuffed me and led me into the van. Cunningham slammed the door behind me and I walked to the back and sat down next to Danny.

> **A cop grabbed my arm from behind, twisted it, and threw me against the police van.**

After a few minutes, I heard my name being called. Finally, through the dirty back windows, I spotted my friend Chip waving his arms. He told me he would call my mom and tell her what happened. "OK," I yelled back, nodding my head up and down just in case he couldn't hear me.

My boyfriend Andrew got thrown into the van, then a kid named Dave. He landed at my feet, crying in pain and unable to see because he had been maced (after he had been handcuffed, he told me). Dave lay on his stomach with his hands cuffed behind his back all the way to the police station.

W hen we got there, the cops opened the sliding door and Dave rolled out of the van and landed in the street. The police taunted and cursed him as he lay there.

An officer named Kohlar led me inside and walked me through a big room with a lot of cops sitting at desks. We went up some stairs and along a corridor lined with small holding cells. An officer unlocked the large metal door and I stepped inside. No one had yet read me my rights, or told me what I was being charged with.

My friends Helen and Cathy were already in the cell. Helen had a large bump on her head from being whacked twice—once with a walkie-talkie and once with a billy club. She said the second blow knocked her unconscious for a few moments. When she came to, she was in handcuffs and her eyes were stinging from mace. The mace had still not worn off and Helen was crying. There was a sink in the cell where she could have washed her eyes out, but we were all still in handcuffs.

Fifteen minutes later, a female officer took us downstairs, one by one, to be searched. I was the last one to be removed from the cell. The female officer took me to a room with bare cinderblock walls. She uncuffed me and told me to take off my jacket and boots. She told me to lean up against the back wall and spread 'em.

She frisked me, then took my jewelry, house keys, and a favorite necklace from my jacket pocket and put them in a little bag. She counted my money and gave it back to me and then filled out some papers which Cunningham, the arresting officer, had to sign. They never gave me a property slip so I could retrieve my belongings after I was released. That was the last time I saw any of my stuff.

Helen, Cathy, and I were taken to the main office and sat on a bench next to the cell that held Danny and Dave. Danny's face looked a little better, but now Dave's face was bleeding. He said an officer had smashed his face into the corner of a soda machine as he led him into the station.

Andrew and another guy named Joey were cuffed outside the cell. They were both 15 and considered juveniles, so the cops couldn't put them inside. Soon the cops took Andrew and Joey into another room and cuffed them to a heating pipe. At around 1 a.m. their parents came and they were both released.

The five of us who were left sat for hours doing nothing. While we were there they brought different people in and out. First was a man named Miguel who was arrested for hopping a turnstile. Then there was a guy who was arrested for selling crack and then trying to bribe his arresting officer. And "Psycho-Loco" had been arrested for fighting. He sat alone in a corner of the cell holding a tissue on his bloody right hand and growling at the other males.

We were each allowed one phone call. I called my mother, who had already heard what had happened from Chip. I thought she'd be angry but she took it really well. She said the police had told her there was nothing she could do, that even if she came down they wouldn't let her see me. She said I was going to be charged with two felonies—riot in the first degree and assault—and they were going to put us through the system.

There was nothing we could do to pass the time except talk about our situation, the cops, and two cute boys inside the cell. Then we started taking about how pathetic we were— we'd just been arrested, and we were still checking out guys! Occasionally a song came on the radio that we liked and we would sing along.

One by one, they took us to have our fingerprints taken. We were seated in a big room with a lot of desks. About eight or 10 cops, both in and out of uniform, were sitting around doing paperwork.

After a while they decided to pick on us. The first insult came from a short, bald cop with a light brown mustache and wire-rimmed glasses. He told Cathy, whose head was shaven except for bangs in the front, and who had thick black circles painted around her eyes, that he wouldn't like to wake up next to her in the morning.

We knew it was pointless to talk back, that it would only make our time there more unbearable. Instead, I just rolled my eyes at the cop's comment about my friend, slumped back against the wall, and rested my right boot on the lower bar of the holding cell. A tall police officer with short, dark brown hair noticed the way I was sitting.

"Look," he remarked to his fellow officers with a smile, "she's trained, she opens right up for me."

I wanted to murder that man, but I knew that's exactly the reaction he wanted, so I just made a disgusted expression. He went on to say that the three of us were whores and needed Lysol between our legs.

I was praying that my lovely visit to the Ninth Precinct would come to an end.

inally, at about 4 a.m., they cuffed us again and drove us downtown to Central Booking.

During the process of checking in I had to get strip-searched. One more humiliation. The female guard searched through my clothes. Then she made me do the old "squat and cough" routine to make sure I wasn't concealing anything inside one of my orifices. I was allowed to put my clothes back on and was led to the large holding cell where I would spend the next day and a half.

It was a 20 x 30 foot space. There was a toilet, benches lining the walls, and two pay phones. Cathy, Helen, and I crammed ourselves onto one of the benches. Most of the other 40 or so women in the cell were sleeping, but a few were quietly talking or just staring into space.

Florescent lamps shone down on us and there were no windows. I had no way of knowing whether it was night or day, sunny or rainy. If my watch said four o'clock, I couldn't be sure if it was a.m. or p.m. The cell was also extremely hot.

We chatted for a little while and made phone calls home just to check in. We decided to try to get some sleep. I don't know about Helen or Cathy, but I couldn't sleep a wink that night.

I spent the next 12 hours befriending crackheads and prostitutes. Then it started to smell really bad and they moved us all to another cell. It wasn't until late Monday afternoon—almost 48 hours after we were arrested—that they took us out one by one and brought us through a long passageway to a courtroom. There I met my lawyer, a middle-aged woman who was appointed by the court to represent me.

During the process of checking in I had to get strip-searched. One more humiliation.

She said the whole thing was ridiculous and that I would be released, but would probably have to come back and appear in court later on. I could see my mom sitting on the other side of the courtroom. I had to wait for around 20 minutes while they arraigned other people, then they called my name.

The prosecuting attorney asked for a "restraining order" to keep me out of the area covered by the precinct. The judge seemed annoyed, like they were wasting his time. He said no to the restraining order and announced that I would have to return for a court date in January. Finally, I was allowed to go home.

In January, the court date was postponed until March. At that hearing the charges were finally dropped because the police had failed to complete certain paperwork within 90 days of the arrest.

When I tell people my story, one of the most commonly asked questions is, "Would you do anything different?"

I would still stick up for my friend. But I would try to watch my back a little bit more and I probably wouldn't yell back at a cop the way I did. But hey, what can I tell you? I didn't have time to think about what I was doing or the consequences of my actions. It all comes down to good old fight or flight, and I wasn't going to run away and desert my friends.

I never really trusted the cops, not even as a small child, because of hearing about corrupt police on the nightly news. When my grandmother's store got ripped off and she needed their help, they never seemed to come through. After my arrest, whatever respect I had for the police was completely gone.

I think there needs to be a complete revamping of our police force. I don't feel cops should be allowed to hassle people for making too much noise or drinking a beer on the sidewalk. And are we really any safer when cops beat the hell out of teenagers or sexually harass 16-year-old girls?

Gia was 16 when she wrote this story. She later graduated high school and went to college, majoring in journalism.

Melanie Leong

What to Do if You're Stopped

By Phillip Hodge

A little while ago I was walking past a few kids who had been stopped by some cops, and the kids were saying, "We didn't do anything. Why are you messing with us?" I thought to myself, "They should just be quiet and stand there. Listen to what the cop has to say and then he'll go away without any trouble."

Many teenagers say they get stopped by the cops for "doing nothing." In New York City in 2009, more than 575,000 people were stopped by the police, and most were let go with no evidence of wrondoing. Not everyone is willing to stay quiet when he feels he's being treated unfairly. But as long as you might end up getting stopped, here's how both cops and teens advise you to deal with it:

G abe, 17, a senior at City-as-School High School, said that when he gets stopped, "I do whatever they tell me to do and try to talk politely, as much as I can."

He said he was stopped by a cop last summer while in the park with his friends. The cop asked him, "What are you doing? Why are you here? Do you have anything on you?" Even though he felt he was being harassed just for hanging out, Gabe kept his cool, and eventually the cop left them alone.

"Unless you want to get arrested, never talk back," Gabe said. "They'll respect you more and it will get them off your back quicker."

The cops I spoke to said that when teenagers are stopped with their friends, they often will give the cops a harder time.

"They'll put on a show, talk back, walk back and forth saying, 'Why you stopped me? We didn't do nothin'!' to show their friends that they're not scared to speak up to the police," said Officer Tyler, a youth officer in the 52nd precinct in the Bronx. But this kind of behavior can get you into even more trouble.

"You should always cooperate," Tyler said. "Listen to what the cops have to say. Don't start cursing and talking back, even if you feel like you are being treated unfairly."

Tyler also said that you shouldn't put your hands in your pockets. "That makes the officers nervous that you have something on you," he said.

Teens who stay calm are less likely to get in trouble, cops said.

"When kids are stopped, they should comply and let the cops do their jobs," said Officer Corr, the youth officer from the 71st precinct. "Avoid any negative and aggressive body language."

When suspects act nervous or aggressive, the cops get nervous and are more willing to be aggressive for the smallest reason. "We always have to look out for our safety first," Corr said.

Both cops said teens who talk back often end up getting searched because they seem suspicious and can even be charged with resisting arrest.

"Even when they weren't being arrested, they'll bring it on themselves by assaulting the officers or by talking back. That leads to a search and, most likely, we'll find something on them," Tyler said.

I t can be hard to follow these guidelines, especially if you feel you've been stopped for no reason.

Vlad, 18, who lives in the Bronx, said he's been stopped several times when he was late to school. "I hate when cops stop me for no reason. I be going to school and they call me over. By them stopping me they're making me more late," Vlad said.

Vlad told me that when he's stopped, he just stands there and answers their questions. But the last time he was stopped, Vlad said the cops accused him of yelling and told him to lower his voice.

"I didn't even be talking loud, and they make it seem like I'm yelling at them," he said. But if I know Vlad, chances are he was yelling. That may be part of why the cops gave him a ticket that time.

In the spring when the weather starts getting nicer, the cops said they stop many kids who are on the street when they should be in school. Teens who stay calm are less likely to get in trouble, they said.

"We'll ask them why aren't they in school, and most of the time they'll give a good explanation that they're late and they are going now, and they talk nicely," Tyler said. "Other times we will get attitudes and curses. That's when we'll bring them to school and give them a cutting slip. You see the difference? It depends on how the person reacts."

Phillip was 19 when he wrote this story.
He later attended college.

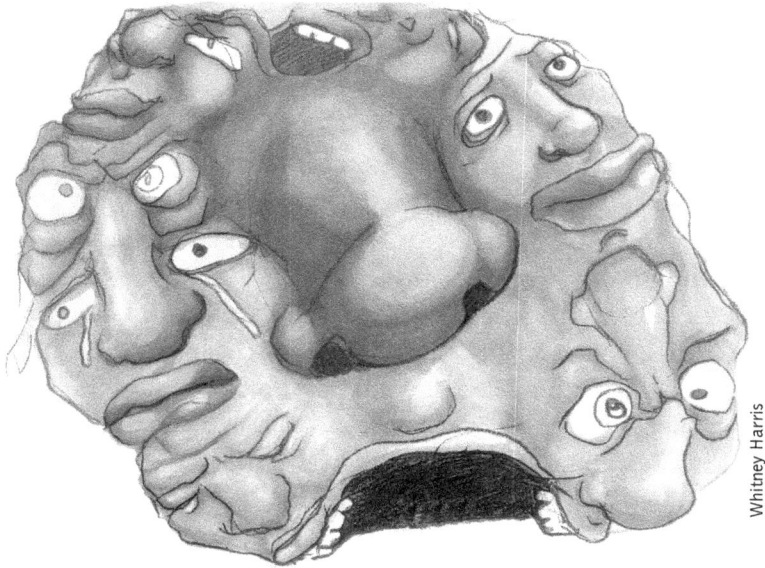

Whitney Harris

Loose Cannon

By Fred W.

"How do you plead to the assault, Frederick?" I looked up at the judge who held my life in his hands.

"Guilty," I squeaked, tears falling down my face.

The judge told me that because I'd told the truth and pleaded guilty, he was giving me a shorter sentence. (I learned the hard way that if I didn't get with the program, my short sentence would grow and grow.) He sent me to a lock-down facility in upstate New York until the state could find me a residential program with anger management.

"Your Honor, can I give my son one last hug before he goes?" asked my mother.

"Permission granted."

She gave me a hug and then I was taken out of the courtroom into the unknown.

Rage led me to that courtroom. My rage started when I was 4 years old and my father started sniffing cocaine. His cocaine use and my parents' drinking led them to fights that became an all-out war.

Here's a typical fight: My good-for-nothing father calls my mother a whore because some guy in the bowling alley told my mother, "You look good! Why are you with a deadbeat?"

At home, my brother and I sit on the couch while all hell breaks loose. My parents look like the old Tom and Jerry cartoons when Spike beat up Jerry in a tornado of fists, legs and screams.

Once, my mom pulled a kitchen knife on my father. I covered my brother's eyes and watched in horror as my father egged my mother on. She stabbed my father in the chest four times, though not deeply. It was so horrible that I passed out.

It was terrifying to experience my parents' violence. The damage they inflicted on each other made me fear them both. Then my father started to abuse me physically and sexually. My fear turned into a rage that consumed me and burned all who tried to reach out to me.

At 13, I was quiet and shy. I pretty much kept to myself. But because of what my father did to me, when I got angry I went straight into a rage.

That year, someone spread a rumor in the school that I was going to shoot a kid named Zeko with a shotgun. I don't know why the rumor spread—hate, jealousy, whatever. Zeko believed it, which I thought was funny at the time.

One day I was coming out of school with some friends. We were slap boxing when Zeko walked by and said, "Take Fred's head off!" I believed Zeko was out to get me. "Crap, Zeko is plotting something and it's my funeral!" I thought.

As I was walking home—fast—Zeko popped out of a large crowd and swung at my face. CRACK! He knocked my tooth out and flung me against the fence. I got up and pulled out the knife

I often carried. Soon I gave up my chase and went home, holding my tooth in agony and defeat.

For the next few weeks, I lived in constant fear. I was afraid my attacker lurked around every corner, waiting to strike again.

A few weeks later, we had a school dance. I was having a great time with my friends until I saw Zeko on the other side of the gym, grilling me with what looked like seething hate. I grilled him back and flipped him off to see if he was gonna pop off.

He walked over and flinched at me. I was scared but thought, "There are mad females here. I can't look like a punk. Plus, I don't want to be hit again." Using my messed up logic, I hit him.

I just meant to shock him, but once I hit him, I blacked out. I didn't feel or see anything until a friend pulled me off. Looking at Zeko, I saw his bloody, lumpy, and bruised face.

My friends told me, "Get out of here before security gets into the gym." Three friends took me home. I was confused and mad. "Why the hell did you help me with the fight? I could have handled Zeko myself!" I yelled.

"Fred, you did that yourself," one friend told me.

"Really?" I asked, surprised and impressed with myself. "Boy, revenge is sweet!"

After that night, I pushed the fight out of my head. I still couldn't remember hitting Zeko, and I didn't know he was seriously injured. But a few months later, the police came to my school and arrested me.

I thought I'd be let go. It was just a fight. The severity didn't hit me until I got charged with assault and locked up. My mom dropped off my clothes at the facility I would call home for three months while I waited for my trial. After that, she visited me only a few times—just enough to keep the courts off her back. (Once they learned about my home life, they were threatening to charge my mom with neglect.)

For the first two weeks, I cried myself to sleep. Even though my family life wasn't good, I missed them and couldn't comprehend living apart from my family for so long. I felt very alone.

After the trial, I was placed in a psychiatric center. I was enraged, thinking, "Why am I here? Please, someone help!" Eventually someone did help, but it wasn't the help I wanted.

That summer, I got transferred to St. Mary's, an all-male residential treatment center on Long Island, outside of New York City. I went to school, took anger management classes, ate, and slept. Anger management classes really sucked. The staff tried to get us to talk about our feelings, but in my family there was an unspoken contract not to talk about feelings, probably because our anger and sadness would have been too much to deal with.

I thought the questions the staff asked about my crime were corny.

"Fred, why did you hit the kid?"

"I was happy, what the hell do you think?" I said. Never again did I talk in that group.

I saw myself as a struggling young man trying to handle my life. The facility saw me as a danger to the community because I was a loose cannon. Since I wouldn't deal with my feelings in the group, the staff figured that I'd beat the crap out of anybody who said something wrong to me.

I was only supposed to be at St. Mary's for one year. But because I wouldn't participate, the judge kept extending my placement, from one year to two, then three, then four. My fourth year at St. Mary's was rough. The staff kept telling me that if I didn't talk, the judge would send me upstate to a tougher facility. That came true. At 17, I got sent to the Goshen Residential Center, a sugarcoated name for jail—razor wire, locked doors, control officers, and a real threat of getting beat up.

Goshen was serious. It made me ask myself, "Where am I headed in life? To prison? I'm about to turn 18. I need to get my mind right so I can get out of here and succeed in life." After about a month in Goshen, I decided that there was no point in fighting the system anymore.

I'd always heard the saying, "Fake it till you make it." A fellow resident at Goshen explain to me the benefits of faking the treatment: 1) people would trust me and let me have privileges, and 2) I might actually feel better.

In groups, I began to talk, thinking, "I'll give them what they want to hear." But I felt relieved once I started to speak about how I felt being away from home and stuck in jail, and feeling that my mother really didn't give a crap about me. As I talked, the residents and group leaders looked at me like they were seeing a ghost.

The group's topic every day was anger, which I didn't like, so I asked if we could bring up other topics. The group leader liked the idea, and from then on the group was open, which made it easier to talk. I started to talk about my feelings of abandonment, fear, and betrayal, and how my past affected me on a day-to-day basis. The group leader and my peers gave me a lot of support, and I began to trust them.

Letting out some of my emotions was the best thing I've done. It helped me find out who I was. It felt great to break my family's taboo against talk-

> *Letting out some of my emotions was the best thing I've done.*

ing about our feelings or discussing what happened inside our house. Telling my secrets, I felt like I was rebelling. Pretty soon, you couldn't get me to shut up.

It's too bad it took me three years and the prospect of getting sentenced to an adult prison to open up. Once I did, I understood why St. Mary's and the judge wouldn't let me go home—I was a really angry guy, and going home to my family wouldn't help me.

Once I understood that my anger and my past were controlling me, I began to try to control my anger. I learned some methods to control my temper, like counting, deep breathing or my personal favorite—pleasant imagery. (I'd think of the best looking girl I knew and imagine locking lips with her. That always calmed me down.)

At Goshen, I also got into creative writing and poetry. Putting my experiences down on paper helped me fight my inner demons. Writing became my self-medicine.

Still, as with all recoveries, it was hard to change. At times, my anger got the best of me. In the facility, there were always guys playing too rough or badmouthing each other. In the past, if someone did that to me, I would have waited for the staff to open up the rec room and popped off without a thought.

Once I understood that my anger and my past were controlling me, I began to try to control my anger.

I had to practice calling a time out inside my head, counting to 10, or thinking about my best friend. I also learned to space out when someone was talking to me in a way I found disrespectful. If someone started talking reckless, I stopped listening and stared into space. Or I'd walk away, put on my headphones, write some poetry, or draw pictures to focus on my own thoughts. All of those strategies helped calm me down.

When I turned 18, I had to leave Goshen. Things got real hectic because the courts didn't want me to go home, but couldn't find a place for me to live. Then I got the answer to my prayers. A group home in Manhattan would take me in.

Before I left for Manhattan, some staff gave me two last tricks to handle my anger: they taught me how to knit, and how to restrain people without hurting them. The knitting helps me feel calm when I'm by myself. The restraining comes in handy if someone's threatening me or hits me, and I don't want to hit them but feel nervous about just walking away.

I was delighted that I was finally free after almost five years. But along with my freedom came some great temptations.

Soon after getting out, I got back into smoking cigarettes and now I'm addicted again. I got caught up in the drug game as well, smoking weed, which I had always loved. Lots of guys in my group home smoked and I wanted everyone to like me and think I was cool. I also just wanted to get high. I love that giddy, spaced out feeling weed gives me. It almost cost me my freedom, though.

Weed made my anger rise, and when I smoked, I didn't want to stop it. When I was high, I didn't care if I got locked up again. Soon I was fighting at least once a week, over stupid stuff like someone bumping into me. I also started robbing people to have money in my pocket, or because I felt angry just from being high.

The cycle kept repeating: Fight, weed, anger, fight, weed... and so on. I had so much going for me but I almost blew my freedom on weed.

Finally, my probation officer did a drug test on me and I came up positive. He sent me to The Realization Center, a program that runs outpatient groups for people with drug problems.

The groups help me so much. We talk about how our drug problem is affecting our lives and how to stop the cravings. Now, after a few months, my cravings are down to a minimum and my anger is getting back in check. I haven't fought or smoked weed in three months.

I've gone back to my good habits—the space out, counting to 10, knitting, poetry, and creative writing.

I think keeping my anger under control is going to be a lifelong struggle. But at least now I'm focused on my future again. I don't want to give up my freedom for anything. I love it too much. When I want to fight or smoke weed, I remember how good it feels to walk to the corner store and buy a bag of chips whenever I want. The girls make freedom worthwhile, too, because in the facilities there were no females (besides the old staff). Plus, I have family that I don't want to lose again.

I've seen so many of my friends go back to jail. But I don't really fear I will end up doing more time. I've changed a lot, and I have too many people in my corner to lose this battle. A lot of staff have given me second chances, and have put their faith in me. I hope I can make them proud.

Fred was 19 when he wrote this story. He earned his GED and worked as a newspaper deliveryman.

Erika Faye Burke

Frontin' for Respect: Life at Rikers

By José R.

What's up, man? You wasn't getting up 7:30 in the morning in New York. But if I don't get up now the C.O. will be by my cell in about five minutes and then I'll have to answer to him. Man, if he ain't have that badge on his chest he wouldn't be nothing. If I was in New York…

Damn the world, damn this place and everyone in it. Got to brush my teeth, wash my face, and comb my hair. Got my fly clothes on. Got to show brothers I'm living large. Yup, got the fly kicks on too. I'm looking proper.

Time to walk out for school. Hold up, let me just flex in the mirror right quick and make sure everything is in the right burner. Can't go nowhere without my burner. Just in case a brother try and front. Alright got some brothers checking me out. How do they do it?

Oh yeah, just keep your arms pretty much still. Don't swing 'em, just move your shoulders and bop to the side a little. Yeah, now you got the walk, let's work on the face I'm gonna wear for the rest of the day. OK, keep your jaws tight, squint your eyes a little. Now, drop your eyebrows. That's it. I'm on a roll now. Man, am I a trooper or what? Yeah, that'll put fear in their heart. They won't even look at me no more. They better not.

Yeah, now you got the walk, let's work on the face I'm gonna wear for the rest of the day.

Man, I hate walking in damn line, like we're in grade school or something. We're passing another house. Look hard. You ain't new to this. A little more on the walk … right, riiight. What's that? Cell block 11? Man, them brothers are crass! Get ready, if any jump off, just keep swinging. Keep on looking hard. Yeah, they know better. Our house is the chop shop. I really could do without the riot squad though.

The riot squad. Man, listen … if I was in New York …

Man, these teachers be buggin' out. What I need to know all this geometry stuff for? As long as I can count my money, I'm straight. Man, what I need to come to school for anyway? I wasn't going to school in New York. Well, I was, but it sure wasn't for no geometry—them girls was fly. These teachers be looking good, too. Man, if I was in New York …

Good, it's time to go back and eat chow. That's just the word to describe it. Chow. Chow-chow is more like it. They must be buggin' if they think I'm gonna eat this. Besides, that lady C.O. over there looks kind of good. If she sees me eating this it'll cramp my style.

Man, I shot 50 bags every week in commissary. Moms be looking out. Yeah, I know things are kind of rough at home, but I'm her son. She can't dis me like that. Yo, the C.O. looked at me. Yeah, you know I look good. I'll take her out for some steak any day, 'cause man if I was in New York …

Man, I hate locking in for this count. Four-thirty, time to lock out. Right on time. Oh yeah, I'm gonna watch cartoons today, and if those brothers change the channel we'll just have to get it on. Yeah, you better not change that channel, 'cause when I was in New York …

What's that new jack with the fly kicks on? He's gonna have to hop out of them. Let me send my little man to get them, 'cause if I got to take this razor out my ass, man, listen …

Look at him—he's scared to death. Yeah, that's it, give up them sneakers. Man, that jacket looks kind of fly too. Naw, I'll leave him with that at least. Herb. But if we was in New York …

What time is it? Yup, it's about that time for me to get up on the phone. Yeah, you see me coming, get up off the phone. What? Oh, calm down baby, he only asked for one more minute. Man, I was ready to blow something. I'll give him that minute, but if we was in New York …

"Hi, Ma. Yeah, I'm okay, how are you? Good. Well, Ma I just called to see how you were doing. Are you coming up to see me tomorrow? Ma, put some money in my commissary. About $50, alright? Yeah, Ma, I know you need to pay the bills, but I need money too. Okay, then the sneakers, right? No, I don't want Reeboks. I wanted Nikes. Forget it! Just bring the sneakers. Ma, I gotta go, okay? Love you. Bye."

Why do these guys have to be all in my face when I'm on the phone? At least they know I get what I want. 'Cause when I was in New York …

Man, this day went by crazy fast. We had some dog food for dinner today again. Man, I couldn't even eat it and I was type hungry. If that guy didn't get cut in the mess hall, maybe I could've at least gotten a chance to eat my rice. That dude cut him up bad, too. At least 30 stitches right next to his eye. Not but four yards away from me either. I seen it coming, too. Thought he was coming for me. Would have cut him right back though, 'cause when I was in New York …

Man, I hate watching the cell door close every night. Be

locked in like some animal. I ain't no animal.

"Yo! Y'all stop yelling out your cells. I'm trying to go to sleep." Bunch of cell gangsters. It's kind of a relief though to have this door closed behind me. At least now I know I'm safe. Ain't no razor cutting through that.

Almost forgot to pray. Lord, thanks for keeping me safe. I could have been the one who got cut, and man was I scared. I could feel myself shaking while we were on the wall. I'm glad no one else saw me though. I thought they were gonna pick me for a herb. But they didn't. Thanks for that too. I know I did wrong when I took that guy's sneakers, but they were all looking at me when I came in the day room. You know, all my friends waiting to see what I would do. I'm really sorry though. I gave him another pair and they weren't that bad.

Why do I feel that even if I'm acting this way, I get no respect?

Lord, I hate having to act like a gangster, but if I don't then I'll be nowhere with no respect. But Lord, why do I feel that even if I'm acting this way, I get no respect?

Lord, my mother seemed pretty upset today. I really hurt her. I wanted to tell her how much I love her and not to worry, but my mans was around me. I know they were listening to my conversation, I had to keep strong 'cause I know she would have made me start crying and that would have been it.

Oh Lord, I'm so scared. I'm so lonely. I don't know what to do. I want to go home. Please, God, if you let me go home, I'll stop selling drugs and stuff. I'll stop acting like a gangster. God, please. Amen. Good night.

What's up, man? You wasn't getting up 7:30 in New York …

At the time this story was written, José was attending school at Riker's Island, the biggest jail in New York City. The story was originally published in STREAMS, a yearly anthology of student writing published by the Waterways Project of Ten Penny Players. www.tenpennyplayers.org

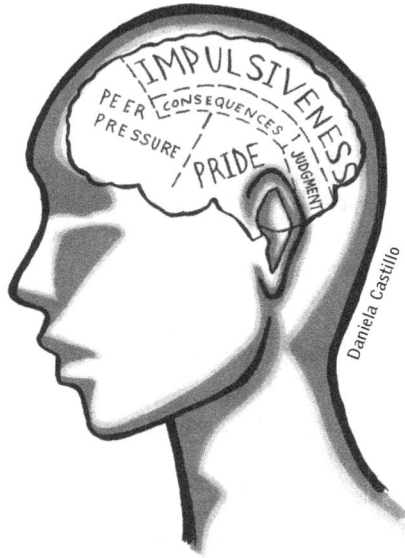

Daniela Castillo

Crazy Kids?

By Anonymous

Nearly everyone has the potential to kill somebody. On one scorching summer day I actually came close to doing just that.

I was 16 years old, playing basketball with an acquaintance. We were cracking the usual, childish, "your mother's so fat" jokes on each other.

They weren't the kind of jokes that should lead to a fight, but they did. He said something about my clothes, I said something about his sneakers, and we both got angry. Soon there was a crowd of kids around us, egging us on. After every joke they would "Ohhhh!" or say, "Yo, you just gonna let him thug you?" We both took off our shirts, ready to fight. I felt like I had to prove myself to everyone, to show that I had heart.

I punched him in the face a couple of times, and broke the skin on my fist from hitting the square of his chin. Then I backed up and fell over a bike onto a bench, and he jumped on me and punched me four times in my face. I had too much adrenaline to really feel the punches, but I was cognizant of the force of the fist hitting my head.

I was dazed when I got up and my head was throbbing, woozy, and heavy. He had given me a pear-shaped knot on my forehead. "Damn!" I thought to myself, "I really want to hurt somebody right now."

I could feel myself getting angrier, and my pride felt damaged. I was humiliated; everyone was laughing at me and pointing at the knot on my head that was visible from outer space. I felt like I had to redeem myself in violent, dramatic fashion. My ego-mind coerced me to say aloud, "If you're still here when I get back, I'm going to stab you."

I ran upstairs full speed and got one of my mother's big Ginsu knives. I ran outside with no self-control, and luckily (for me and for him) he wasn't there. There was a crowd of kids that scattered when they saw the knife, though. I stood there for a few seconds with the knife in hand, and saw the scared looks on people's faces as they fled. In that moment, I felt like I was the knife, dangerous and lethal. I felt powerful.

With no one to fight, I went inside and threw the knife away. I looked out the window at the scene I had made. Someone had called the cops and there were two uniformed police officers walking through.

I wasn't really angry anymore, and I wasn't scared that the cops would come looking for me. I was just there. Everything felt so surreal that I didn't know what to think. My senses had failed me, especially my common sense.

This is just one example of a time in my life when my impulsivity overcame me. I realize now I wasn't using "the good brain God gave me," as my mother would say. Instead, pride resided in my brain, and it was a tumor the size of a fist.

Apparently, though, it might have been more than just pride

that kept me from thinking straight. Scientists say that teenagers' brains are great at learning but not so good at controlling impulses or recognizing consequences.

Teen brains are like "a car with a good accelerator but a weak brake," Laurence Steinberg, a Temple University psychology professor, told the Associated Press. I know that for me as a teen, it was hard to stop going down an impulsive, destructive path once I was on it. During that fight on the basketball court, some girls who didn't want to see me fight had urged me to back down, but it barely registered. "Don't fight him, it's not worth it," they said. I put that through the rinse cycle for two seconds, but I still shrugged at my conscience.

I was humiliated. I felt like I had to redeem myself in violent, dramatic fashion.

These differences between teen and adult brains are especially important in dealing with crime. In 2005, for example, the U.S. Supreme Court had to decide whether it's appropriate to give the death penalty to someone who committed their crime before the age of 18. The American Psychological Association argued against the death penalty for juveniles, saying teens' brains haven't matured enough to control decision-making, so they shouldn't receive the same harsh punishment as adults.

They also argued that a teen who's violent or makes stupid decisions won't necessarily always be violent and impulsive. They might grow out of it and not be a danger to society. "Adolescent risk-taking often represents a tentative expression of adolescent identity and not an enduring mark of behavior arising from a fully formed personality," the Association told the court. In the end, the Supreme Court did outlaw the death penalty for juvenile crimes. And in 2010, the Supreme Court also outlawed life sentences for juveniles for all crimes except murder.

Not thinking about or fully understanding consequences is also common among teenagers. During the fight, I didn't think about my own well-being or anyone else's. I could have killed somebody. I didn't give that a second thought, nor did I think about the police, my mother, or any other consequences.

Research has indicated that teens have a difficult time making judgments because the frontal cortex of the brain, where decisions are made, is actually undergoing physical changes during adolescence. That development can affect the way teens behave and the choices they make. I think brain development, as well as teens' lack of experience and wisdom, are important to keep in mind when sentencing teenagers.

Scientists say that teenagers' brains are great at learning but not so good at controlling impulses or recognizing consequences.

Teens should be handled with special care.

To the adults who say that these studies about teen brains are just being used as an excuse for teens to get off easy, I say that I'd like to take a time machine back to their high school or college days. There is a good chance that these same people may have been smashing cans of beer on their heads or doing other dumb things. As my great-grandmother says, "The old was once young."

Even after reading about the teen brain, it's still hard for me to understand my actions at 16. (I'm 21 now.) I can only imagine what could have happened that day if the other kid had still been there when I returned with the knife. I might be in prison and he might be dead. Thankfully, that didn't happen. I did see the kid around sometimes, and we would give each other dirty looks, but it never escalated to blows. And I never did anything that bad again.

In the last few years, I have gone from being an angry and sometimes violent person to being a peacemaker, perhaps thanks to my more mature brain. These days, even when provoked, I'm pretty good at keeping cool. Most recently, I was with a female friend when some guys made rude comments directed at her. I could have gotten really upset and escalated the situation, but instead I just stood between her and them and ignored them, and they stopped.

Even though I wanted to punch them in the head, I was able to control my impulses much better than I did that day, long ago, on the basketball court.

The author was 21 when he wrote this story.

William Pope

Confessions of a Shoplifter

By Norman B.

"Yo, that's a nice shirt. How much you pay for that?"

"Man, please, I ain't pay for this. I stole this!"

I can't count how many times I've said that to some of my so-called friends.

"Yo, you should take that. Ain't nobody lookin'. Go ahead. What, you scared?"

And I can't count how many times they've said that to me. And I don't want to.

I always feel bad when I think about the fact that I fell into that trap, thinking that if I stole I'd be considered cool, or down. Little did I know the only thing anywhere near cool was the fact that I was doing something illegal, which is cold. And the only thing that went down in that situation was my name on a police record.

Yes, I admit it, I used to steal. But it's not something I'm proud of. And if I had to explain why I stole, I guess I'd say it was for many different reasons.

When I was a lot younger, I always got everything I needed and wanted. I was the first grandchild to be born on either side of my family, so it was natural that I was adored. Whether I needed a new winter coat, money for school, or a new pair of sneakers, I got it. And because of all that I became spoiled and developed an attitude of entitlement. Even after I became a teenager I still felt that I deserved to get what I wanted, when I wanted it, no matter what.

But when I was about 12 years old, my family had some serious financial problems. My grandmother was laid off from her nursing job. My mother was going to school and working part-time. Because of that we had to go on public assistance.

It was very embarrassing, and I felt like hiding, or disguising myself any time my mother and I went into the grocery store and she'd use food stamps.

It was like we'd hit rock bottom. I knew it wasn't my family's fault—they had to do what they had to do to survive. I could see how depressed my mother and grandmother were over all this, which made me feel even worse.

But I was also angry at them and felt they should be ashamed of what was going on.

So I still asked them for money, and I didn't want to hear them say no. When they refused, I would throw a tantrum.

The people I hung out with never seemed short of cash, and this made things even harder for me. Besides that, we used to be called nerds because we were smart. But I didn't like being made fun of. So finally I decided that I'd make sure I got what I wanted my own way.

I stopped hanging out with my old friends and started being friends with the other kids. You know, the "in" crowd, the ones considered to be mad chill. Those were my so-called friends who introduced me into the dead-end world of stealing.

We'd hang out at the malls looking at all the clothes and CDs we'd get if we had the money. I'd watch all these other kids walk out of the store with the things they wanted, while I stood there and daydreamed, with just enough money to catch the bus home.

I'd think about what I wanted my life to be like when I became an adult. I had already promised myself that I wasn't going to be poor. I told myself that once I started making money I'd buy myself a beautiful house, and have a BMW and a Mercedes pro-filin' in the driveway. But as I stood there watching those kids, I felt lousy, and mad as a bull. That's when my friends and I started to steal.

We used to steal all kinds of things. Shirts, jeans, sneakers, and CDs. One time a girl actually paid me $40 to steal some sneakers for her. Sometimes if we got hungry and had no money we'd go to a store and steal cookie dough, potato chips, lunchmeat, and whatever else we could get away with.

Every time I stole, I'd feel a little nervous about being caught. But because I was friends with the "in" crowd, I couldn't show how scared I really was. I just brushed my feelings aside and played off being cool. Sometimes I felt a speck of guilt. But not near enough to make me stop. I didn't think that much about the people I was stealing from. Mainly I just figured that since it was a store, I wasn't stealing from anyone.

Sometimes I felt a speck of guilt. But not near enough to make me stop.

And after I'd steal, I'd get this big rush. I'd feel superior because no one had caught me. In my head, I'd say to the security guard, "I can't believe you're so stupid! I just put a CD in my pocket right in front of you and you didn't see me!" I'd feel relieved that I'd gotten away with it, again, each time that I tried it. And I'd feel powerful and free.

Stealing was like a high, an escape from my problems at home, and from reality. Because I had to concentrate so hard on not getting caught, I didn't think about any other problems. I felt bad about my life, and the only time I felt a little better was when I was stealing.

ike any addiction, I wanted that feeling to last. I wanted to feel free and superior all the time. Even getting caught didn't stop me from stealing.

One day I was in the mall with a new friend of mine. We decided to go steal some CDs. We each had a couple and were walking out of the store when, out of nowhere, the guard came up to us.

Then he told the both of us to empty out our pockets. That's when we knew that we were caught. He escorted us to the back of the store, told us to sit down, and played back the video where they recorded us stealing. I never felt so scared in my life.

After that they took pictures of us and made files with our names on them. They handcuffed us and escorted us downstairs on the escalator, which they stopped just for us. When we got to the police station they told us to call our parents. When I asked, "What happens if we decide not to call them," he said that we'd have to go to the detention center until Monday. So I called my mother. After that the police handcuffed us to the seat.

When my mother came, she was angry. "What the hell is your problem?" she said to me. But I could tell that more than anything else she was hurt.

I was assigned a probation officer. They thought this would keep me from stealing. But the next day was like the rest, and I continued to steal. I was caught two more times after that incident, but nothing much happened. Mainly I was just told not to come back to the store. And I kept on stealing.

By the time I was 15, there were lots of other things going wrong in my life. My father was in jail, I was fighting with my mother and other family members all the time, and I was failing in school. I was sent to live in a group home, and then to another one.

When I first arrived, I'd try to steal whenever I got the chance to go out. It didn't matter if it was candy, food, clothes. Anything, as long as I stole something. It was the only thing that made me feel better.

But over time, my life began to change at the group home. I started talking to a therapist, getting out some of my anger. And I began to improve my life. Eventually, I developed a reputation for being smart, and many of the workers at my home were proud of me.

I liked the feeling of doing good things and being recognized for it. That began to be my new high. And I felt that if I continued to steal I'd be a total fake. Plus, I started going back to church. One Sunday when the reverend was preaching, he spoke of the Ten Commandments. One of them is "Thou shalt not steal." When I heard that, I was really shaken. So I started praying, asking God to forgive me and help me change all my ways.

At first it was hard for me to stop because I would see so many things I wanted that I knew I couldn't have, and I hated that. One side of me would ask, "Why didn't you steal that CD like I told you!" But the other side would say, "Norman, think of what could happen if you get caught."

I'd try to think how I'd hurt my mother all over again and jeopardize my future. And that would make it easier to resist. After a while I didn't have to use that method anymore because I no longer wanted to steal.

Now I've got a part-time job, and when I want money, I earn it.

Still, in some ways, I haven't changed. I have expensive tastes and I'm still a materialistic person. I like to have money in my pocket. Only now I've got a part-time job, and when I want money, I earn it. Sometimes I become impatient when I have to wait to buy something, but that's what makes me want to get it even more. Before, I was addicted to stealing. Now I'm addicted to working.

I don't like to ask people for money when I'm more than capable of earning it myself. I want to be able to buy myself the best.

But that's not the only reason I like to have money and nice things. It's also because too many times I've heard people tell me that I wouldn't amount to anything. I want to show them how wrong they were.

I know that I already have amounted to something. And I don't even believe that if you don't drive a BMW or own a big house you haven't succeeded.

Still, I've always had this little feeling that I may not make it in life. And in some way I feel that if I make a lot of money, everyone will see how they misjudged me. They'll see that I have made it, working, not stealing. And they'll see that I did it on my own.

Norman was 16 when he wrote this story.

Stefan Vaubel

Brick Walls of Justice

By Bönz Malone

The glistening neon of 42nd Street in Manhattan lit up the sky like the Star Spangled Banner. Everything was there: The pimps, pushers, hustlers, and smut merchants. Buying and selling souls, just like that—now you see them, now you don't. In the blink of an eye they're gone. The only ones left were Finsta and Shanks, my amigos from Broadville.

After we met up on the corner of 42nd and 8th, we went searching for biddies—me to interview, them to skeeze. The avenue was like a ghost town, as if we were the only survivors of a new generation.

It wasn't till we got to 48th that we saw a kid coming up the block. We had just got finished drinking a 40 and were whistling the Woody Woodpecker song.

As he came closer, Shanks asked him, "Where's the girls'

group home at, money?!"

The kid, who was a pizza delivery boy, stuttered to answer.

Finse, who had that look in his eye (you know that look—something's gotta give and it might as well be you), was getting ready to hoist the kid on a bum's rush. I felt it too, but what could I do? I live with these guys; if I punk out, my rep is dead. Fortunately, the kid ran, so no attempt was made on his life.

Still on our mission to find that female frat house, we walked down 48th to 9th Ave. Suddenly, a long arm called the law grabbed me from behind.

"Get that *#@and%! over here, punk! Lookin' for gold?"

"Leggo," I said.

"Shut up, punk!"

"I said leggo!"

Breaking free from his grip, I jetted six blocks, eluding four squad cars and a jeep. Finally apprehended by a civilian, I was turned over to the men in blue.

Frisked while handcuffed, I was unable to stop them from stealing my watch and gold money clip. They hauled me in the ghost wagon.

"What's your name, bastard?"

"Rubber duck!"

Pow! That was smart. Because of my quick tongue, Officer Schlepp gapped me in the chops.

After the joy ride, I met up with the guys at the station.

"Yo, what happened to you, B'zoe?"

"I got bagged."

"Damn, you look messed up."

"I'm all right."

That night we spent in the bullpen, cracking jokes and smoking cigarettes, acting like we were three-time losers. The bullpen was about 60' ft. by 25' and was jam-packed with derelicts and evildoers. One guy threw up on himself and was left to stink up the cellblock.

The highlight of the evening was the synthetic bologna

sandwiches. We'd trade ours for candy and C.I.'s (cigarettes). We didn't make night court, so we had to sleep in a dirty cell where they would bury dead produce.

The nights were long and the tears were silent. If you were heard whimpering by the C.O.'s, they'd haul your butt down to P.C. (Protective Custody) and bust your head open with the jimmy. So quietly you sleep, weep, and wait for your release.

The next day they came for us. Me, Finse, and Shanks were shackled together, while they took us to another location.

"Yo, where are we goin', man?"

"You're goin' to the Tombs, kid."

"You mean we're gettin' the chair?!" someone said.

"You'll see."

After a hearty oatmeal sandwich, they took us back to the courthouse we had come from. I thought the nightmare was over, but it was just beginning. At about 2:30 p.m., they split us up. Finse went to another room and Shanks disappeared.

"Now," I thought, "I'm going to find out what jail is really like."

In the Tombs (a jail in lower Manhattan), they feed you like a king. Sometimes you get a room with a view and other times you couldn't get a room. I crashed on the hard ground and smoked my cigarette. The sorry faces, smelly feet, and unfriendly attitudes made me sick to my stomach. But I was cool and I didn't let it get to me—till...

"Yo, shorty, gimme a C.I.!"

"Aye yo, I ain't your shorty and you ain't gettin' nothin'!"

"So what's up?"

"My temper!"

By now, the guards could hear us, but couldn't care less. I was on my own, alone to fight for my name Malone. Before he could make a fist, I floored him with a chop to the crotch.

"Take that, punk!"

This excited the others, causing them to call me whatever

name I desired. Although scared like hell, I learned not to take no shorts, and I was prepared to do whatever necessary to survive in the Brick House.

That night I was transferred to the Rock (Riker's Island jail). Half conscious, we arrived at the gate. Inside we were strip-searched and then we took showers.

"Don't drop the soap, shorty, we're watchin' ya!"

"Your mutha!"

"Whatchoo say?!"

"I said, go jump your mutha"

"I'ma getcha, shorty!" is all I heard while I was walking away.

Back at my bunk, I sat up thinking about my mother and why I was being held on attempted robbery charges at $1,500 bail. And if that wasn't it, I hadn't been given a phone call in three days! Although I wanted to cry a thousand times, I kept my self-control. I needed my strength to overcome this test of endurance.

The highlight of the evening was the synthetic bologna sandwiches.

As I sat on the edge of the bunk, someone tapped me on the back. I jumped.

"Calm down, troop. You want a stogie?"

"Look, man, if you're giving me the stogie 'cause you're cool, then gimme one and step off. But if it's a piece of ass you want, then kiss mine first."

"Here's your cigarette, kid."

"No strings?"

"No strings. What's your name, money?"

"Bönz Malone, The Unknown."

"I like your style, Malone." He stretched out his hand. I gave him a pound.

"J.J. Dillin, House Gang Krue. Where you from, Malone?"

"From the world of ruff crews, 718."

"Yeah, I'm from Brownsville."

"I'm from Crime Heights."

For a moment, there was silence. Each of us thinking about something to say and how to say it.

"How did you get a name like Bönz?"

"My mother gave me that name. It's short for Business OrgaNiZer."

"But can you get busy?"

"What the hell is that supposed to mean?"

"You'll see."

Dillin and I spent most the night shadow-boxing in the can. He was of stocky build and very defensive. There were no hacks (C.O.s) around, so we were free to exchange elements of style. From Southpaw to the famed "Peek-a-boo," he showed me his philosophy of "a raw deal."

But the most important thing he taught me was to accept responsibility for one's actions.

"If you throw a punch, then you deserve to get your feelings hurt! Have you taken a good look at this place? This is the system's way of fighting back."

"Don't worry 'bout it. I'll be all right."

"Yeah, that's the same thing my brother said. My brother was a hustler, in with the wrong crowd. Until one day he stepped outta Fort Greene Projects and the same people who he was hustling shot him in the head five times. I told Fifty to slow down, but he wouldn't listen."

"Your brother was Fifty Cent?!"*

"You heard of him?

"Everybody knew that dude—he was a bad mamma jamma! But ain't nothing like that is gonna happen to me, 'cause I ain't going out like that!"

"Yo, you cool and the whole 10 yards, but you talk that ol' fast s--t, and if you ain't careful, someone's gonna put your lights

---

Kelvin Martin, a 1980s Brooklyn stick-up man, whose nickname was later adopted by the rapper Curtis Jackson.

out!"

With a look of pain, he went back to the tier. I knew it wasn't because of the workout. If anything, I was the one that felt like a bag of crushed ice. I sat for a moment and wondered to myself: "I thought he was cool. Why did he come out his face like that? Maybe he sees something in me that helped carry his brother to the other side."

All this was food for thought, and speaking on food, I was starving like McFarland. Yet, it was late, so I went to bed.

For some strange reason, Dillin and I became the best of friends after that pep talk. Awaiting parole, I started hanging with a motley crew known as House Gang. I figured, while in there, I oughta pull my weight. I was in charge of mopping the tier and detail distribution.

For breakfast, Cookie made his usual—menthol mush.

"What are we having today, cook?"

"The usual."

"Again? Fooey!"

"What kind you want? Halal or Kosher?"

"What's the difference?"

"Kosher comes without the ashes!"

"Sounds great, but I pass."

"Suit yourself, kid."

The mess hall was filled with mouths to feed. All you could hear was the sharpening of teeth and the sound of guts digesting. Meanwhile, back at the ranch, the hack was calling me.

"Malone...Bönz Malone!"

I got word from JJ. to gear up, 'cause I was leaving on a jet back to the courthouse. Fortunately, it was a come-as-you-are party, so I was all set to go.

On the way to the limo, Dillin was waiting by the door.

"Ya got everythin'?"

"Yeah, I'm straight."

"I hope so, 'cause if I see you back here again, I'ma kick yo ass!"

As I shook his hand, I knew that mutual respect was being handed down to us.

"I like your style, Malone."

"Take it easy, Jay."

"However I can get it."

As I got on the bus, I felt a part of me cry out in sadness, knowing that the greatest lesson I ever learned was due to the worst experience I ever had—behind the brick walls of justice.

After explaining to the Judge, I was granted parole with a date to come back in the summer. When I left the courtroom, I knew that I had endured the test of courage, and after a long embrace from my mother, I cried.

Bönz was 20 when he wrote this story. He worked as a columnist for magazines including Spin and Vibe, and appeared in several films, including White Boys *and* Slam.

Daniela Castillo

Who Gets a Second Chance?

Before the late 1970s, juvenile justice laws were fairly lenient in most parts of the country. In New York, for example, if you were 15 years old or younger your case would be heard in a special court and you couldn't be locked up for more than five years, even if you'd murdered someone.

But in 1978, a 15-year-old named Willie Bosket murdered two people on the subway. He had already built up a long rap sheet and when people realized he would be free in five years, a public outcry followed.

New York State politicians were eager to change the law to show they were tough on crime. One option would have been to introduce what some other states had at the time: a "transfer up" system allowing judges to move dangerous juvenile criminals into regular adult courts on a case-by-case basis. A teen transferred to an adult court would face tougher punishment.

New York went further than that. Suddenly, children as

young as 13 and 14 who were accused of certain serious crimes were required to be tried in adult courts. They faced mandatory imprisonment and a permanent felony record.

Judge Michael Corriero, who was on the bench from 1988 to 2008, heard many of these cases—for a while, he was the only judge hearing the cases of 13- and 14-year-olds being tried as adults in the city. It was up to him to decide whether a kid should be locked up or get "youthful offender status," which allowed the kid to receive probation and be sent to an alternative-to-incarceration program. "I had the responsibility of deciding who went to jail and got a felony record for the rest of their lives, and who got a second chance," he said.

We talked to Judge Corriero about how he made those decisions. We found he believes courts should "protect and nurture" children and teens who are able and ready to change for the better, as he wrote in his 2006 book, *Judging Children as Children*.

Here, in his words, is some of what he told us about juvenile crime, peer pressure, and hope:

There was a 14-year-old African-American girl, we'll call her "Loretta," who was riding the subway with her friend. The friend is a little bigger and tougher than Loretta. They're sitting across from a young lady who has beautiful, shimmering earrings. The friend, who's a bully, says, "Look at those earrings. I want them."

The bully gets up and Loretta gets up with her, and they hover over this girl. The bully says, "Give me your earrings." The girl tries to walk away, but is blocked by Loretta. Again the bully demands the earrings; no response. The bully rips the earrings out of the girl's ears. Train doors open, and there happens to be a police officer standing there who charges the bully and Loretta with robbery in the second degree.

Loretta got up with the bully, knowing that the

bully wanted the earrings. Therefore, she faced the same punishment as the bully: imprisonment of a minimum of one to three years and a felony record, unless I granted them youthful offender status. Both came before me, and I found that Loretta had never been in trouble before.

I told one of the alternative-to-incarceration program representatives who used to come to my court, "Interview Loretta. Tell me what you think of her." The representative asked her a typical social worker question, to get a sense of who she was: "If you could change three things in your life, what would you change?"

Loretta said that she would change her country, because she believed

If you have no hope, how are you going to find the strength to walk away?

America was a racist society; her family, because her mother was a crack addict and she never knew her father; and her sex, because she felt that young women were vulnerable to physical and sexual abuse.

How do we make Loretta believe she has the power to change the circumstances of her life? If you have no hope, if you feel that the world is an obstacle for you to realize your dreams, then you have nothing to grasp onto when you're standing there surrounded by your best friends who love you, who take care of you and protect you, but who nevertheless want to do something very bad. How are you going to find the strength to walk away?

What I tried to do, with Loretta and other young people I thought I could work with, was to place them in alternative-to-incarceration programs where they could learn to better appreciate their self-worth and the opportunities that existed for them.

Barack Obama's second book was *The Audacity of Hope*. "Audacity" is an interesting word. It's like you've really got to overcome something to hope. That's what Loretta needed to be able to say to the bully, "I can't do that; it's not me; it might jeopardize my career or going to school." That audacity to hope.

Of all the kids that came before me, I put about 65% in alternative-to-incarceration programs. Of those, about 17% got re-arrested during the course of that year. It was 17% too many, but of the kids that I had to send off to lockup—the kids I couldn't give a second chance to, either because they were very violent or they'd had numerous chances before—60% to 80% were re-arrested within six months of their release from the institution. So the system is failing young people in lockup.

It's going to be up to your generation to bring about all the things I want to see happen: going back to a "transfer up" system; making sure that all the kids we have to send away are educated and given the kind of mental health services they need; making it so that, even if I have to give you a felony conviction, if you stay out of trouble for 10 years, you should have a way of coming back to court so that we can seal your record. Because if you have a felony record, your life is so curtailed.

How would you like to be defined forever by what you did at 13? To me that's not moral; it's not fair.

Editor's Note: Judge Corriero's comments have been condensed and edited for clarity.

YC Art Dept.

Alternatives to Jail

By Madeline Legister

Minors who are charged with a crime are sometimes sent to "alternative-to-incarceration" or "alternative-to-placement" programs instead of juvenile prisons. The goal of these programs is to create a healthy environment in the child's life and to teach young people how to control themselves, while also teaching their families a better way to do things.

There are several different kinds of alternative-to-incarceration programs. For example, there are Functional Family Therapy programs, in which a therapist meets with the family of the young person in their own house, usually once a week for about five months. This type of program helps the family members learn to trust and listen to one another. This sort of family intervention can sometimes help a kid stay on track.

Other types of alternative-to-incarceration programs remove

the young person from his or her home. For example, in one program run by the Cayuga Home for Children in the Bronx, juvenile delinquents live with "host" parents for nine months, away from their real parents. The host parent is trained to enforce a set of rules. The teen must get signatures from all his teachers to prove that he went to school. The teen is not allowed to see his real parents or go home unless he shows that he's following all the rules.

Sometimes, a judge might prefer to send kids to alternative programs like this rather than jail if it seems like the young person just needs another chance and more support. Alternative programs can also be a lot cheaper than sending someone to lockup.

Although they're becoming more popular, these programs do have limitations. Some of the programs do not take kids who have been abusing drugs, who have mental illnesses, or who are sexually aggressive, and some programs only take kids who have a family member willing to participate.

Madeline was 17 when she wrote this story.

John Gaston

My Life as a Thug

By Patrick A.

Last year, I was hanging with a few associates who I thought were my homies. We were all broke, bored, and joking around that jacking would put money in our pockets. I said, "Yeah, let's jack somebody. We need the money so we can start grinding."

We said it so much that finally we went and did it. There was a group of four of us. We approached a young man and I said, "Pocket check, n-gga. Give me your f---n' money right now." Then my friend hit him and we took the guy's money, then jumped him and took his bundle of weed.

When we were done I did feel bad for the person we jacked. But I also felt good that I could come up on $40 or $50. I guess the feeling good part won out because after that we kept doing it.

We wouldn't take just money. We would take clothes, jewelry, shoes. We would go up to people and tell them, "If you don't give me what I want, I will beat yo ass." There were people who'd fight to protect their stuff, and I can understand that. But when they wouldn't give us their stuff, we would beat them up. We would jack people five, six, even seven times a week. None of us had jobs and this became our way of making money.

The sad part is, after that first time, I didn't even feel anything when I was jacking people. Really, the only thing I felt was, "I'm the man." I felt proud, like a higher authority who could command what I wanted. It didn't matter to me about the people's feelings. It only mattered what we were out to get.

Before I started jacking people, I wasn't a trouble child. I was going to school, making good grades, and I was on the j.v. football team. I was a leader on the team, mainly because I always hustled, play after play.

I didn't care about our victims and I didn't care much about where my own life was headed either.

But in between football seasons, I began to feel that there was nothing much that mattered. On and off in my life, when things weren't going well, I'd get an "I don't care" attitude. I went into foster care when I was 5, and that attitude would kick in whenever I felt I had nothing special to live for.

When I was a kid, I didn't have either one of my parents around, due to physical abuse, financial problems, drug addiction, and neglect. But for lots of years I did have foster parents who cared about me. And when I was jacking people, I was living at a group home where I had staff who cared about me. All those people really did try to do their best for me.

But something inside me felt like no group home staff or foster parent could ever substitute for my parents. Sometimes I used that as my excuse for not caring.

So when my friends and I started jacking people, it was easy for me to get into that "I don't care" mindset. I didn't care about our victims and I didn't care much about where my own life was headed either. And once I started messing up, it just led me further down the road of destruction. I was messing up at my group home too, not following any rules.

But for a while, the more we did it, the better we felt, going from nobodies to somebodies just by making ourselves a bad reputation. People who knew me would say, "That n-gga is hard." They'd say it about all of us together, our crew.

Then I'd look at the goods that I got from the victims—money, shoes, chains, watches, rings, even drugs a couple of times—and that felt good. It felt good to ball, to get my hustle on, to make ends meet. Before, when I didn't have the money to buy what I wanted, I'd walk through the stores and be envious of the people who could.

And the OG's (original gangstas—the men I'd looked up to growing up) had always told me to be a productive man, and I convinced myself that's what I was doing. They said legal or illegal, there's money to be made. They said illegal should always be my last solution for how to survive. But they said if there was no other way, then making money illegally was better than being a bum.

After a while, we took the money we made from jacking people to buy and sell drugs. Today I often ask myself why I kept putting the bad element back into our community. At the time I was just thinking about the money I was making and the power I had..

But soon my attitude got me arrested.

None of my homies got caught and all the people we jacked described me as the head person, the one who would be the most intimidating. None of my so-called homies were there to back me up. That was a blow. I thought these guys were my true boys, but when I landed in trouble, I found that really I was alone.

I started to realize that the trouble I was getting into was just not worth it. While I was out on bail awaiting trial, my group home made sure there were consequences for what I'd been doing. I was on punishment all the time, not going anywhere with my friends, not being able to use the phone, not receiving any allowance. The school took away my breaks and lunches and isolated me from my friends and teachers during time off.

I had been proud of my reputation in front of the other kids, but now I was ashamed that my teachers saw me as a thug and a bully. All of it made me say, "This isn't the road I want to go down. This road will hinder my future and lead me to do hella time in the pen."

I really only started thinking about the people I hurt when I went to court and had to pay restitution. It was only $50, because in the end, they only managed to find enough evidence against me in the case of one person I jacked. But I did see all the codes and files and all the charges, and that caused me to feel some regret. A n-gga can't pull a low down dirty gangsta move on an innocent person and expect never to feel any regret.

I thought these guys were my true boys, but when I landed in trouble, I found that really I was alone.

Mainly, though, getting arrested scared me straight. I think I'm lucky that I didn't get locked up, because I really did do a lot of low stuff, and I'm sure the people I robbed and hurt think I belong behind bars.

Still, for about the past four or five months, I've been changing my mentality. I'm trying to do well in school and my new group home is helping me find internships and learn ways of making legal money for my future.

I received six months probation and 60 hours of community service, and I've been keeping my nose clean. I've even been keeping my 10 o'clock curfew. I have plenty to remind me not to slip up: like having to take piss tests, having my probation officer check up on me even in school, and basically not having my freedom.

But I've begun to feel better about the situation I'm in, in part thanks to the help that I've gotten from people in foster care. I feel like if I keep on the path I've started on, I won't be a failure in life. It's a good thing that I finally woke up to reality.

Patrick was 17 and living in San Francisco when he wrote this story.

William Pope

What's the Charge?

By Max Morán

On a February night at 1 a.m., those who are supposed to serve and protect me kidnapped me. My friend and I were walking home after he bought two forty-ounce beers, and I decided to carry one of the bottles for him. His plan was to drown his troubles with his two favorite friends—the 40 and me.

But half a block away from my apartment, two plain-clothes cops confronted us. When we passed their parked car, one of them stuck his head out the window and asked me, "What's in the bag?"

"Just beer," I said.

"Where's your I.D.?" he asked.

I said I didn't have I.D. because I was not expecting to use it. Then the cop said, "You're the only person I know who walks around without I.D."

My friend told the cops that it was his beer and that he was 21, so there shouldn't be a problem. Next thing I know, we're being searched and handcuffed. By then I was in total shock. I'd never been in trouble before. "I wasn't expecting to get arrested for carrying a brown bag," I thought to myself. There I was handcuffed like a criminal, wondering what had I done wrong. We weren't even read our rights.

They said they were taking us to the precinct to make sure there weren't any outstanding warrants for our arrests. But before they put us in the car, the officers opened both beer bottles, poured some of the beer on the street, and then put the bottles back in the bags. "That's odd," I said to myself.

At the stationhouse we were herded into the bullpen where there were already five people sleeping on the floor. The officers said that the computers were down and it would be a while before they could check for any outstanding warrants.

That cell was full of people who hadn't taken a shower in days and it smelled like pure funk. I ignored the stench the best I could. When I saw those people curled up on the floor I vowed I wouldn't do the same, but after four hours I was too exhausted to care. So I sat down on that dirty floor. Carrying unopened beer bottles in a bag isn't a crime, even if you're underage. There I was, sitting in a dark corner and asking myself, "What's the charge?" I wasn't even allowed to make a phone call.

From there they took us to another precinct, where the arresting officer, Ken Dayley, fingerprinted me. When he finished he said, "You did good, I'm proud of you."

I didn't know what he meant by that. I thought about what he said for a while and now I think he was proud of me being arrested and fingerprinted—the first steps that could lead to a life behind bars.

Officer Dayley took me to another room and told me to empty my pockets. I found an unfamiliar folded paper in my pocket. When I took it out and looked at it, Mr. Dayley yelled,

"Put that $^#&$^# down!"

Cursing back at him crossed my mind, but I knew that the less I said to him, the better for me. I knew he wouldn't be yelling at me if he didn't have that gun. I gave him a dirty look. At that time I would have done anything to have Mr. Dayley drop his gun and fight fair with me. In that state of mind, I don't think Mike Tyson could have whupped me.

Next stop was another cell to be strip searched. That was the worst I've felt in my life. It wasn't fun having a man look at my private parts.

From there I was held in another cell until 7 a.m., when I was to be taken downtown to see the judge. During the hours I was in that cell, I finally realized why the cops opened the beer bottles and poured them on the street. They needed an excuse to arrest me—drinking in public.

It's funny how you miss all the little things in life when you're locked up. Like walking down the street, or sitting somewhere watching the pretty girls go by.

At 7 a.m, 19 of us were chained together and put in an armored truck for a ride to the criminal courthouse. I remained quiet, too pissed off to say or do anything. All my life I'd been concerned about doing the right thing, but now I was trapped. I was missing my apartment. I wanted to be home working out and listening to music.

It's funny how you miss all the little things in life when you're locked up. Like walking down the street, or sitting somewhere watching the pretty girls go by. Being in that truck was awful. A couple of times I closed my eyes, hoping it was a dream and that I was really home watching T.V. But when my eyes opened, I found myself chained like a slave.

At the courthouse I was strip searched again and fingerprinted twice, then put in another holding cell. I sat staring into space, waiting for my date with the judge, one of hundreds of suspected criminals, all complaining of being wrongly arrested.

How could all of them be lying? And was it a coincidence that for every white male, there were 10 blacks or Hispanics in there?

As time went by, my urge to get out of there grew. For lunch and dinner they gave us salami sandwiches, and we had all the tap water we could drink from the cell's sink. I didn't eat anything.

Also, I hadn't slept for over two days. I took a little nap here and there but I needed to keep my eyes open just in case. At night guys fought over cigarettes and sleeping places on the floor. With this madness going on around me, I realized prison life doesn't adjust to anybody. You must adjust to it.

I got to see the judge at around 12:30 a.m. The court's lawyer informed me the charge against me was drinking in public. She advised me to plead guilty. If I did, I would be released that same night and maybe end up with a little community service. And the case would be thrown out.

I told her I was innocent and wanted to clear my name. She said that if I pleaded innocent, I would have to make bail money and fight the case in court. It would be my words against Mr. Dayley and his partner (two white police officers). I knew who the judge was going to believe.

I looked down at my hands. They were dirty from being fingerprinted so much. My clothes and body smelled funny. I wear contacts, so my eyes were burning. And, worst of all, my pride was hurt.

So I pleaded guilty (which I later regretted), and was released that night. They told me that if I stayed away from trouble for six months, my case would be thrown out.

If I had known the way the system works, I never would have pleaded guilty. If the charge was drinking in public, I should have demanded a blood test to prove that I hadn't been drinking.

Why did Officer Dayley arrest me? Why did he frame me? He knew that the beer bottles weren't open and that we weren't drinking in public. He tampered with evidence when opened those bottles. Maybe he arrested me because he needed the overtime hours or more arrests on his record.

But then this cold chill comes over my body. Maybe Officer Dayley and his partner are racists. If not, what were they doing in their car in a black and Hispanic neighborhood, looking for anybody who, to them, seemed suspicious? If they aren't racists, why did they frame me? They could've given me a citation and sent me on my way. Instead, they arrested me. Maybe they wanted to see a Hispanic man suffer.

I've been a God-fearing, law-abiding man, and look where it got me in your world. I played the game by your rules. I trusted you. Yet the first chance you had, you took full advantage of me. You chained and handcuffed me like some wild beast.

You may say I shouldn't be walking around with beer in a paper bag. But you shouldn't be sitting in a car waiting to kidnap people at will. To us, we are dressed comfortably. To you, our appearances look suspicious and every one of our movements is dangerous. That's why you're so quick to lock us up or shoot us in the back.

Those 23-and-a-half hours behind bars made me lose respect for the system. Every time I see a police officer, the first word that comes to mind is "pig." I don't like feeling this way, but I can't help it. It's unfair that one police officer can ruin the reputation of many others who wear their uniforms proudly and who truly serve and protect people.

Since Officer Dayley arrested me without a charge, it's only fair that I use my freedom of speech and charge him. I charge Ken Dayley with kidnapping, tampering with evidence, and disorderly conduct. I charge him with overstepping his boundaries while using his badge as a shield.

How do you plead Mr. Dayley? Innocent, you say? I find you guilty as charged.

Thereby, I sentence you to 23-and-a-half hours behind bars. You will be arrested without a charge and no one will read you your rights. You won't be entitled to make a phone call, and you will be strip-searched and fingerprinted three times. You will be yelled at, handcuffed, chained, and forced to ride in an armored truck. I want you to feel like a caged animal, the way I did.

How do you, Officer Dayley, sleep well at night, knowing that you arrested an innocent man? We both know I'm innocent, yet, in your world, I'll always be guilty.

Max was 21 when he wrote this story. He later graduated from college and graduate school and became a social worker.

'Dignity and Respect'
America's model youth justice system is built on empathy

By Jan Nicole Garcia

One evening in the early 1970s, Mark Steward—then a group counselor with the state of Missouri's Division of Youth Services—took his group of juvenile corrections kids to Pizza Hut for dinner. When he said hello to a young woman in the restaurant, the kids noticed.

"They said, 'She's good-lookin', man! Why don't you ask her out?'" Steward remembered, laughing. "And I said, 'OK, I think I will!'" The woman eventually became his wife. "If it weren't for the kids in Youth Services, I probably wouldn't have been married these past 38 years," he said.

But the kids in Missouri's juvenile justice system also have many reasons to be thankful for the system Mark Steward helped set up in that state during his career. The story he tells about Pizza Hut illustrates the kind of relationships that kids in Missouri's juvenile prisons have with staff and with each other.

That kind of relationship, one of "dignity and respect," is

what Steward considers the most important part of the "Missouri model"—what people now call Missouri's approach to juvenile corrections. In 1970, Missouri had what Steward calls a "horrible" juvenile justice system and was trying out a new, softer approach with a few of its toughest juvenile prisoners. Steward was just out of college and was the first counselor hired to work with them.

Before, these kids had been locked in cells and made to wear prison uniforms. The new approach was different: no more locked cells, and kids could wear their own clothes. Also, "We dealt with them more as a friend and a big brother or big sister, and came to them from a personal connection instead of a position of power," Steward said. After a few years, the kids were doing so well that the whole state of Missouri began switching over to the new method.

Steward eventually rose to become the director of the state's Division of Youth Services. The state received national attention for the success of its methods. Today, Steward runs the Missouri Youth Services Institute, a nonprofit organization that advises other states' juvenile justice agencies—including New York's—on ways to improve their systems.

These are kids who made mistakes; they're not bad kids. We all deserve a second chance.

It makes sense that other states would want to adopt the Missouri model. Of youth released from Missouri's juvenile prisons in 1999, 70% had avoided returning to a correctional program three years later; nationally, the success rate was as low as 25% in places.

Because of this, Missouri's system has been called "the Missouri miracle," but the reasons for its success seem obvious. Missouri's juveniles are placed in small groups of 10-12 kids who spend all their time together and support each other. There are many juvenile prisons throughout the state, so kids stay close to home. They have well-educated adult counselors who listen to them and try to help them reflect on what they've done and why they did it. Family therapy helps them improve their relationships with their families. When they eventually return home, they're given a lot of continuing support.

Despite all these services, Missouri's system is not especially expensive—it's about in the middle between the least expensive and most expensive systems in the U.S. So why isn't everyone using the Missouri model? Steward said it comes down to being "stubborn or stupid."

"In some cases it's hard for them to admit that they've been doing the wrong thing for years and years and years," he said. "A lot of people are arrogant, power-hungry. And that doesn't sit well with saying we've been having problems, we need to change."

In some cases, adults just don't like to see kids looking happy and comfortable in juvenile prisons. Juvenile justice administrators from one state actually told Steward that kids should be treated badly so they wouldn't want to come back.

"What we always thought was, it's punishment enough to be sent away from home. What these kids need is help," he said. Because many kids in prison have been through physical, emotional, and other trauma before they got into trouble with the law, "we try to create a healing environment and a safe environment for the kids, so they can figure out how to change their lives."

Often, a teen's biggest obstacle to making positive changes is peer pressure. So the Missouri model uses the power of peer pressure in a positive way. "We try to teach them to not go with the group when the group is going wrong," Steward said. It works most of the time, because compared to adults, "kids are more flexible and will listen to others more. They're less set in their ways."

After interviewing Mark Steward I was surprised to know there are people involved in juvenile justice who really care about youth. His personality caught my attention: He seemed kind, wise, and genuinely interested in making juvenile prisons around the country more humane.

"These are kids who made mistakes; they're not bad kids. We all deserve a second chance," he said. I think it's a good point. None of us are perfect and as kids, we're not always mature enough to know what we're doing. Sometimes we don't think, we act impulsively, and we make mistakes.

However, I believe no one was created evil. Like Steward said, a lot of the kids in lockup have been mistreated. Sometimes kids who are considered "bad" just don't have the support and attention they need, and they confront their feelings by hurting themselves or people around them.

Those kids do need help, and the Missouri system gives it to them. It seems like a place where kids get that care and comfort they never had. By the results, we can see how possible change is with attention and support.

Jan Nicole was 16 when she wrote this story.

Matty DeLuna

A Day in the Life

By Anonymous

I got in trouble with the law last year after I tried to rob some kids, and I was sent to jail on Riker's Island in New York City.

I was 17 and I'd never been in jail before. When I first got to Riker's, I was scared. I'd heard about it from my friends who'd been there. They'd told me that it was crazy and that people were always getting cut in there. I found out my friends were telling the truth.

All the boys were held together at Riker's, and the adults were held together in another part. We had to wake up at 5 a.m. to eat breakfast but that was too early for me to get up, so I never ate breakfast.

At 7 a.m., the C.O.s (our name for the corrections officers) would walk by our cells to do the first head count. If someone was missing, they'd shut the whole jail down until they found the missing person or figured out why the count was wrong.

The cell doors opened at 7:30 a.m. for the kids going to school at Riker's. On weekdays, I went to school from 7:30 a.m. until 3:30 p.m. That was fun because some friends from my old high school were there.

On weekends, I got up at 9 a.m. Then I brushed my teeth and listened to my radio until noon, when the officer would open my cell. While I was waiting in my cell, I felt like a real criminal. I'd get mad at myself, not really for doing what I did, but because I got caught.

Then I went into the dayroom to watch TV with the other boys until 1 p.m., when we had lunch. We usually played cards, chess or checkers, or we'd play fight. We were allowed to use the phones for up to 15 minutes so I sometimes called my grandmother, my mother, or my girlfriend.

But it was hard because I had to fight 10 people to use the phones, which were right by the bubble where the officers were. Sometimes the officers would just watch the fights, but other times they'd stop fights by beating us up and macing us.

I played around with other kids until 2:45 p.m., when we had to go back to our cells. Then I'd listen to my radio and fall asleep until dinner.

While I was waiting in my cell, I felt like a real criminal.

On weekdays and weekends, there was another headcount at 5 p.m. At 7 p.m., we ate dinner in the dayroom. The food they tried to make me eat was a whole bunch of slop with a piece of bread and some milk, so I had a hard time eating it. Instead, my friends and I would make meals from soup, fish, rice, and cheese that we bought from the commissary. (That's where we could buy food when we got money from our families.) I'd also buy Pop-Tarts, popcorn, and other snacks.

After dinner we'd watch a little more TV till 10 p.m. Then we'd go back to our cells. I remembered when my mother used to make me go to bed early, and I felt like a little kid again. The last headcount was at 11:30 p.m. Then we'd go to sleep, wake up, and do the same thing the next day.

About two days after I got to Riker's, about 20 kids ran into my cell and took my clothes, food, and some books. Man, listen, I had to do something about it because I don't believe in turning the other cheek. I ran into the dayroom and started to fight about 10 people in there. You might think I could have told the C.O.s, but snitching could get you killed in jail.

To punish me, the C.O.s sent me to the box, a holding area for the bad kids, for two months. I was on 23-hour lockdown in a small cell with a bed and a desk (no TV). I couldn't come out of my cell except to take a shower. All I did was read books, sleep, and talk or yell at people in nearby cells.

The box was worse than anywhere else. It made me feel like a slave in a cage or someone lost in another world. I survived by eating whatever food they gave me and by sleeping all day. I got out by completing my time in the box with no problems.

When I got out of Riker's, I felt like a kid who was born again. I started making changes in my life. My counselor at the Center for Alternative Sentencing and Employment Services (CASES) got me a job and I'm taking classes at CASES to get my GED. I'm also writing rhymes and working hard to become a rapper.

I spent eight and a half months at Riker's, and I don't ever want to go back. It's not a place any kid would want to be. I'm not hanging out with the wrong crowd anymore, and I'm going to try to do better going forward so I can stay out of prison.

Cezary Ladocha

My Little Bouts With the Law

By Mariah Lopez

Usually people don't want to talk about how kids bounce between the foster care system and the juvenile justice system. For them, it's a matter of saving face or hiding their embarrassment, but for me it's just a matter of fact…being in the New York City foster care system has been a very big factor in my little bouts with the law.

Now, I'm not looking for sympathy. And I won't deny it, I won't make any sheepish excuses, nor will I beat around the bush…I have been a walking terror! My record is, for lack of a better term, lengthy.

My delinquency problems first started when I was 13. I had just gotten out of a large residential treatment center. From there I was bounced around mercilessly from group home to shelter to foster home and back again.

In part this was due to my own dissatisfaction with my placements, the ones that just put too much of a cramp on "my life, my way," and compelled me to run. But usually it was also because of verbal, physical, and emotional abuse from the staff and residents at these placements.

See, I'm transgender (biologically male, becoming a female), and group-home boys can be the worst in terms of being homophobic, picking fights and destroying all my feminine gadgets and gizmos.

Staff were just as bad most of the time, refusing to stop the boys from antagonizing me. They'd just tell me: "You're too feminine, you bring it upon yourself," and, "They called you a fag?…well, aren't-cha?"

I felt like I had found an illicit avenue of escape from my relentlessly miserable life.

It's hard living in places where you just know everyone dislikes you, has all these biases against you or just doesn't care about you. Like most other kids in foster care, I didn't want to let group homes and other foster care placements define my life, so I sought out something totally independent of foster care and its whims—a life of my own.

It was while I was bouncing from place to place that I was introduced to the lively sub-culture of the ballroom scene (voguing and the whole bit) along with all the social, and quite often illegal, baggage that comes with it: prostitution, boosting/mopping (stealing) and lots of drugs and sex with older men. When I found this world, I felt like I had found an illicit avenue of escape from my relentlessly miserable life.

With the drugs it was like, "They're here, I'm here, we're here together so I might as well." Everything else gave me the very real rush of adrenaline, which was addicting. Besides, at the time, within the group of people I belonged to, all these illegalities were not only accepted but praised and glorified.

Eventually, I ended up living in a group home for gay and transgendered males, and I was actually quite content there, contrary to popular belief, or my own ranting and raving and li'l bouts with the staff. Still, by the time I found that place to call home, I was already too deep into the scene to want to get out. By then, those were my people and that was my life.

The first time I was arrested I was hanging out with my girlfriends ready to ambush the next street pharmacist ready to make a sale, and hit it to the club. Suddenly 'Mag' (as we call the cops) were all around us, shouting, "Shut-up, assume the position." We were all charged with loitering with the intent of prostitution and soliciting, and I was taken to a juvenile detention center.

The first issue to arise when I got there was the long black weave in my hair, which, I was told, I would have to remove. When I refused, I was held down and my lovely 12 inches of Janet Body Wave was literally torn from my scalp, as were all my other articles of female paraphernalia.

I felt naked and humiliated. All in all, between the uncertainty of what seemed at the moment like my entire life and the new unfamiliar and unfriendly place, I felt miserably alone.

The next day I appeared in front of a family court judge, and found out that not only had I been arrested, but now my group home (the only place for kids like me on the East Coast) was kicking me out. They said I was just too much to handle. Well this, in part, was true. But I also felt like the only family I had was turning their back on me. I was an emotional mess.

Next the judge gave ACS (the city's foster care agency) specific instructions to find me an appropriate placement—whatever that means. But ACS put me in a group home in the Bronx where I had been three times before, from which I had AWOLed on three different occasions.

Now the house and its program weren't my biggest concerns. It was that blasted neighborhood! There I was on the worst strip of tar-pressed gravel the city calls a street, having to duck bottles, bullets, perverts, and the constant ill-tempered comments of ignorant pedestrian passersby. It just wouldn't have been healthy for me to stay, in any way.

So for the whole month between court dates, I AWOLed almost every day, to a friend's house nearby, or to places far far away. Of course I did take advantage of this self-acquired freedom, attending the occasional party here and there, or storming a club every now and then. But mostly it was just to get away, to get a rest, to feel safe.

So, on the next court date, my judge decided to lock me up in a non-secure detention facility—a group home-like place for kids with non-violent charges. I was there for about a month, and then I was released (paroled) to a friend's mother as a foster parent. But soon enough, I was arrested again for the same charges. (For the record, I was not prostituting, though I was hanging out downtown after curfew.)

The group home said I was just too much to handle. I felt like the only family I had was turning their back on me.

After that, the same judge sentenced me to a year in state custody. Now, I'm not for a minute going to pretend that I was an angel during that year. I did scream and hit staff. But I still don't think I deserved the treatment I got. I was involved in over 20 physical confrontations with staff (not to mention those I had with other residents), I attempted suicide twice, and for 362 nights, I cried myself to sleep. The time I spent locked up (a whole year, shy of three days) was, honestly, the most miserable and lonely stretch of existence ever lived. (The one exception was a truly caring man who was my Language Arts teacher.)

But this story is really more about why I got locked up in the first place than what it was like to be locked up. I truly believe that, because of a lack of emotional incentive to do well, a place to call home, as well as the fact that kids in care often grow up surrounded by crime, we are more at risk of becoming juvenile delinquents or having some brush with the law. For me, it was about trying to find a place where I belonged.

I know that at times some of us, like myself, can seem impossible to handle, totally beyond control. But I still believe that it's the job of the foster care system to figure out how to deal with us without treating us like criminals.

Mariah was 17 when she wrote this story. She has since worked as an activist on her own behalf and for other youth with Amnesty International, the Sylvia Rivera Law Project, and other groups.

YC Art Dept.

Life After Prison

By Tanisia Morris

I always assumed that teens in the juvenile justice system were given lots of opportunities to get their lives together. But recently, three teens who've been through the system told me a different story.

"Once you're in the [juvenile justice] system they're going to try their hardest to keep you until you're 18," said Ashley, 17. "It's hard to get out."

Ashley spent eight months at a juvenile detention facility after getting in a fight. Now she's on probation and living in a group home in Brooklyn. I interviewed Ashley and two other members of Each One Teach One (EOTO), a youth leadership program in Manhattan that educates and trains teens about the juvenile justice system.

"You feel like an animal," said Ashley about her time in

prison. "It strips your whole freedom away. We were locked up—barbed wire and everything."

"I felt like a slave," agreed Antoinette, 17, who spent 19 months in at Tryon Girls' Center near Albany, New York for robbery and assault. She said she felt isolated from her support network. "I was all the way upstate in the boondocks. There was no escape." Her mom had to leave her house in Brooklyn at 4 a.m. and drive six hours to visit her.

Rodney, 18, has also been deeply affected by the system. After being caught with a gun, he was sentenced to six months at the Center for Alternative Sentencing Employment Services (CASES), an "alternative to incarceration" program.

He feels the juvenile justice system doesn't do enough to prevent teens from making the same mistakes once they're released. "There's nothing for them to do when they get out, so they go back to what they're used to," he said.

But Rodney is about to graduate from CASES, which provides juvenile delinquents with education, counseling, internships, and job training under strict supervision. He spent one week at Riker's after missing 10 days of work at his program, and says he'll never go back to jail again.

All three teens are determined to have a positive future. Rodney plans to go to college for business management. He's waiting to hear back from several local schools and hopes to start in January.

He knows it's up to him to stay on track. "It takes self-control to be around the same surroundings you were in before you were arrested, but keep yourself from being a part of it," he said. "Even now, certain things happen, and I feel myself getting ready to slip and I have to catch myself."

Ashley said that when she went back to school after prison, most of the people she used to know were either locked up or dead. Meanwhile, she has set goals for herself. She wants to get her GED and become a paramedic or nurse. Now she's in a GED program and hopes to complete it soon.

And Antoinette's experience in the system actually helped her pick a career. "I used to bark at my lawyers," she said, because they never seemed to defend her the way she wanted. And now?

"I want to be a lawyer to help people," she said, smiling. "That's my dream."

Tanisia was 19 when she wrote this story.
She attended Lehman College.

For information on CASES, see www.cases.org.

Rafael Manashirov

Teaching from Their Mistakes

By Sheela V. Pai

This time last year, Bernard Skelton, 17, was in jail for armed robbery. Now he's making presentations to kids in schools and community centers all over New York City. The main goal, he says, is "to stop kids from doing bad."

"When I was little, people told me 'Don't do this, don't do that,'" says Bernard. But those people were adults. He says he wishes he could have heard from people closer to his own age: "Kids who have been through the same experience."

Now Bernard tells kids about the way he started down the wrong path so they won't have to make the same mistakes. He tells them how his grades started falling, how he was kicked off the basketball team, how he had problems with his family and had no one to talk to.

"I was living day by day," remembers Bernard. "I quit my job because I was arguing with the manager. For two weeks I searched for another job, but then I stopped. I'd play basketball, hang out, and sleep late."

Finally, when he ran out of cash, he turned to crime. "I decided to make money the quickest way possible," he says.

The thing that turned him around, says Bernard, was when he was in jail, reading a poem he had written in which a young man dies. "Do I want to become like the end of the poem?" he asked himself. "I said no."

Like Bernard, Whetsel Wade, 22, also decided to change his life while in jail on Riker's Island. For Whetsel it wasn't the first time he had been in jail. He had lived hard and he'd been shot on more than one occasion-once seven times. "All my close friends were dying," he said.

Whetsel recalls his mother coming to him in jail and telling him, "You're going to either end up with a lot of [jail] time or dead." A few days later, his exit counselor told him the exact same thing. According to Whetsel, in the streets, when you hear the same thing twice, it's the truth.

Both Whetsel and Bernard were referred by exit counselors at Rikers to a program at the Friends of Island Academy, an organization that helps young men recently released from prison get on with their lives. That's when they began making their presentations. "I've been through a lot," said Whetsel. "I don't want [other kids] to go through the same things I went through."

Whetsel talks to kids about how he used to be known for always carrying a gun and how people would challenge him just to look brave. He tells them about what it was like getting shot and about always having to look over your shoulder.

"You may have a nice Lexus from drug dealing," he explains. "But as you're driving by, somebody can shoot you in the head." Instead, Whetsel advises kids to "go to school." Then, he adds, "Get that car and you ain't got to watch your back."

I asked him how he could be sure these presentations were having an impact. "When we enter the room, [the kids] go,'Oh, boy,'" he said, indicating that they were expecting yet another lecture. "Towards the middle, though, I see open eyes and no one talking. Then, after the presentation, they come up and ask 1,001 questions."

Bernard agrees. "At the end of the presentation they will come down and give us their numbers and whatnot," he said. "They'll tell us they want to change and ask us how can they change."

In the presentations he gives Bernard says he tries to focus on the positive. "I try to get them to ask questions about how they can prevent getting into the situation I was put in," he said.

I don't want [other kids] to go through the same things I went through.

Whetsel uses the skills he's learned through the program to act as a "peacemaker" in his own neighborhood. "I be tryin' to tell [kids] the smart thing to do," he said. "They don't diss me or nothin.' "

Whetsel says he has gotten many people from his neighborhood, including some of his old friends, to join the Academy. While in college, Whetsel plans to write a book about his experiences so he can reach even more people.

Both Whetsel and Bernard said they benefit from talking about their experiences as much as their audiences do. "It helps me see things differently," says Bernard. "[Before,] if I had no money, I would have done the same ol' thing. Now, after being associated with [the Academy], I hear my bad side, but my good side overpowers it. If I'm going to preach what I teach, then I should follow it also."

Whetsel feels he has profited from giving presentations as well. "It's straightened me out," he said. "Even if I wanted to do something, I couldn't because I just told those kids not to do it."

Sheela was 16 when she wrote this story.
She later became a lawyer.

Ashay Francis

Get Out and Stay Out

By Fred Wagenhauser

Most kids coming out of detention have a lot on their plates. I know, because I was locked up. When I came out, stress and temptation almost got me locked up again. It was stressful dealing with aftercare workers who would ship me back in a heartbeat, and trying to stay straight in a neighborhood where marijuana was everywhere. Many of us give in to temptation. Then BANG! We get locked up again.

Most of the guys I knew in jail struggled and failed when they came out. I thought my friends were unusual for going back to jail so quick, but I recently found out that they aren't the exception, they're the rule. The recidivism rate (that's the percentage of people who go back to jail at least once after being released) for teens in New York State is 85%. That means that for every

100 kids who leave lockdown, 85 eventually return to jail, going back through the revolving doors of the justice system. Only 15% survive out in the world.

To find out why that happens and what can be done to keep kids straight, I talked to two teens—Shane Correia and Wendy Roman—who are on the Center for Court Innovation's Youth Justice Board. That's a group of teens who spent a whole year studying the problem of youth getting locked up a second time. Talking to them, I was happy to find out that there are people who really care what happens to youth who've been locked up, and that teens are taking a stand on the issue.

When Shane, Wendy, and the other Justice Board members learned how many teens end up locked up again, they were shocked. So they interviewed more than 30 people—teens and adult experts—to find out why and how to fix it. Then they wrote a report and presented their findings to the leaders of the juvenile justice and education systems in New York.

The teens on the Youth Justice Board found three main reasons why teens didn't make it once they came home:

1) Lack of motivation. When youth come out of the system, they have the same anger they went in with, go back to the same neighborhoods and families, and have the same friends they got in trouble with before.

Changing the way you act and think, changing your friends, dealing with your family differently, and turning yourself into a good student are not easy. Not many teens have the motivation to change and few have people pushing for them. So they fall off, get back in the hustle, and get locked up again.

2) Trouble getting into school. Facilities have trouble transferring credits and many schools refuse to take back students who've been locked up, even though it's not legal for schools to do that. Principals are under a lot of pressure to show they're improving their schools. Sometimes they try to do that by keeping out kids who have fallen far behind grade level or who might be troublemakers.

3) Lack of family support. When kids are locked up, their families get used to not having them in the house. Sometimes it's more peaceful without them, and parents don't know how to handle their kids once they come back. Everyone has to readjust. A parent in the Youth Justice Board report said, "It was easier while the youth was away. Now I have to worry how much work I'm gonna miss this time around to go to court or to meet with a guidance counselor because my child isn't going to school."

From my own experience, I agree that those are the top reasons. I'd also like to add three others they didn't highlight:

4) Help dealing with emotions. I got locked up because I couldn't handle my anger. If somebody looked at me wrong, it was a fight. Somebody stepped on my kicks, I popped off. In the facility, I learned some decent ways to handle my anger, but many kids don't get that kind of help in jail, and when they come out, they lose the support groups that kept them stable.

5) Drugs. When I moved to Manhattan, it was hard to walk even a few feet from my building without being asked if I wanted a dime bag. Much as I wanted to be out, I also wanted to feel free, and that meant getting high. When I got sent to outpatient drug treatment, it helped a lot. Honestly, I think lots of teens who've been locked up could benefit from that.

6) No money. Coming out of a facility, it's hard to find work. If their families don't have their back, lots of teens sell drugs for quick and easy money or turn to gangs for support.

I've managed to keep from being shipped, but I have made mistakes. Luckily, my parole officer gave me second chances, and I've learned to dust myself off and try again. I've also been lucky because I was released to a group home in a new neighborhood and found a strong support system. My friends help keep me on track.

But I'm one of the lucky ones. The system can't rely on teens having luck and resilience if it's serious about keeping us out of jail (and saving taxpayers a lot of money).

The Youth Justice Board came up with more solutions to make this flawed system better. Here are their ideas, which I think are great:

1) Motivate young people to succeed. Youth coming out of lockup should go to forums to discuss the temptations of being free and brainstorm how they can make it through probation. Also, youth should get matched with mentors who they can relate to during hard times, and who can give them the attention that their families or aftercare workers may not be able to offer.

Changing the way you act and think, changing your friends, dealing with your family differently, and turning yourself into a good student are not easy.

2) Help young people get into school and stay in school. Before youth leave a facility, they should be enrolled in a school. The school should fit the young person's interests and needs. Some kids need vocational programs, where they might learn to fix cars or run trains, and others need small schools focused on preparing for college. Facilities should also provide workshops to prepare youth for returning to school.

3) Strengthen the relationships between family and youth. When youth get out, their families need counseling and support groups so they can deal with some of the issues that got the kids locked up in the first place and learn how to handle being back together.

What I liked most about talking to Shane and Wendy, and reading the Youth Justice Board report, was that these teens did a lot of work to wake up our state's leaders. They were kids who lived a "normal" life—none of them had been locked up—but were willing to spend time working on a cause they believed in. I thought no one cared about kids in the system and no one wanted to help us. Their work has inspired me to stay straight. I can at least be a role model to other kids in my group home, who are struggling to stay free of the streets.

Fred was 19 when he wrote this story.

For more information on the Youth Justice Board, see www.courtinnovation.org/youthjusticeboard.

YC Art Dept.

Time for Change
Head of juvenile prisons in New York is listening to teens

An interview with New York's head of juvenile justice

Interview by Johane Celestin and Catherine Cosmo

New York's juvenile prisons have been counted among the worst in the world by some juvenile justice advocacy groups. The practices used in these facilities came under special scrutiny in 2006, after an emotionally disturbed 15-year-old boy died following a physical struggle with staff in which they pinned him to the ground. Then, in 2009, the U.S. Department of Justice issued a shocking report that revealed terrible conditions in four of the state's 28 juvenile prisons: Staff had broken kids' bones and knocked out teeth while trying to restrain them. They also reported that there was little real care for teens with mental illnesses and drug addictions. And a subsequent state report said these conditions were common across the entire system.

So, why are juvenile justice advocates feeling optimistic? One reason is Gladys Carrión. In 2007, Carrión was appointed to run the state's Office of Children and Family Services, the agency in charge of all the juvenile detention centers in New York. (As commissioner of OCFS, Carrión also oversees the state's child welfare services such as foster care, adoption, and child protective services.)

Carrión, a lawyer from the Bronx, is a reformer. She's hopeful that all the bad publicity the system has gotten will spur the changes that she believes are urgently needed. We met her at the Bronx Residential Center, where she explained how she wants to improve things.

Q: Why do you personally care about juvenile justice?

Gladys Carrión: I care about the young people very much. In part, I see myself in a lot of these young people. They come from the communities I grew up in. I see my nephew, my son, my neighbor's children in these facilities and in the system.

Q: Some people say that kids who are in the habit of acting out should be removed from their schools and communities to keep them from being disruptive. What do you think about that?

Carrión: I disagree. If we're going to incarcerate anyone and deprive anyone of their liberty, we need to think long and hard about doing that. My position is that you should only remove a young person from their community if they truly pose a danger. Unless they're dangerous, we should find a way to address their behavioral or delinquency issues within the context of their community.

Q: Since you became commissioner in 2007, you've closed or

merged 14 juvenile prisons in the state. Why?

Carrión: One, because we don't need them. We have fewer young people coming into our facilities because counties are increasingly using alternatives to detention (alternative-to-detention programs usually attempt to rehabilitate kids without taking them out of their homes). Also, even if we had enough young people to fill our upstate facilities, I would still close them because they are too far from where the young people come from.

You should only remove a young person from their community if they truly pose a danger.

The majority of the young people entering the juvenile justice system are from New York City, but because most of the facilities are upstate, sometimes parents have to travel five or six hours just to visit their children. From that far away, it is very difficult to engage the community and family, to make those connections that young people and their families will need in order to make an effective transition back into the community.

We're planning an initiative in Brooklyn where we can reuse and retrofit our Brooklyn residence. We're working with Mark Steward, of the Missouri model, who is providing us with some technical assistance on how to redesign our facility and our program. (See our story explaining the Missouri model on p. 74)

Q: What other changes are being made to the state's juvenile prisons?

Carrión: There's a philosophical shift from a correctional model that emphasizes punishment and control to a model that looks at addressing the needs of the young people and their families. So we're changing the environment and the culture in our facilities.

We're working really hard, and I think with lots of success, to reduce the number of physical restraints (like handcuffs), and to improve staff's skills. We're also engaging with families more, and we're thinking about re-entry (kids going home) from day one, as soon as the young person comes in.

We're looking at improving our education and vocational program. In some of our facilities, we're training young people for jobs in the green economy. We're doing therapeutic interventions that address some of the deep trauma many of our young people have experienced to help them understand why they're acting a certain way and to help them set limits for their own behavior.

Q: Where would you like to see New York state's juvenile justice system go from here?

Carrión: I would like to see less reliance on confinement (fewer kids being locked up). I'd like the system to rely more on alternatives to detention.

> *It's important for us to understand that young people have the capacity to change.*

I'd like to see a system that allows young people to work with victims and become more sensitized to some of the harm that their behavior causes. It's important for us to understand that young people have the capacity to change. Their brains are not fully developed yet. We need to understand adolescent development much better and take that into account. Most importantly, I think we need to listen to young people a lot more than we do now.

Also, an area I have absolutely no control over is police practices, but it's an area I think we should look at. Why are so many people being detained?

Q: What are the biggest obstacles you face in reforming the system?

Carrión: There are a lot. In closing facilities, there's been a real pushback in upstate communities where these facilities represent jobs for local people. But I always say that I am not the commissioner for full employment. I am the commissioner for children and families, so that's my priority.

The other challenge is that people are scared of these kids. They think that they're predators and that they need to be far away in order to ensure public safety. The facts do not show that. There has been no spike in juvenile crime because I'm closing facilities and we're using more alternatives to detention.

In some counties, people working in the system are resistant to the idea of alternatives to detention. I had a conversation the other day with one court counsel—that's like a prosecutor—who asked me what we should do with a teen who's noncompliant, who does graffiti once, then twice, and three times, and six times. I asked a very simple question: "Is that young person dangerous?" His answer was no, so I said, "Well, you gotta find another way because jail is not the response."

I cannot see incarcerating a young person, depriving them of their liberty, because they are doing graffiti. And I happen to not like graffiti at all, it gets me upset, but we need to find other approaches to address that young person's fascination with graffiti. Maybe it's art classes or something else, but not prison.

Editor's Note: This interview has been condensed and edited for clarity.

YC Art Dept.

Stories From the Inside

As part of a journalism class inside a secure detention center, three teens wrote about how they ended up there and what life in lockup is like. Here are their stories.

Always in Trouble

By Anonymous

Yo, this is my life and how it goes: I remember being at home around age 3, listening to my mom and dad arguing. I listened helplessly as my father beat up my mother. This happened a lot. As time went on, I became more and more angry with myself. I was also abused and I took it all out on other people since I couldn't fight back against my father at the time. Because I went through abuse, I started to have behavior problems. By age 8, I'd been kicked out of five schools.

When I was 9, the city took me away from my family because I always had bruises and other marks on my body. When that happened, I threatened to take my own life. People asked me why and I told them it was because I was not used to being away from my family. So they decided to put me in Bellevue Hospital, where I stayed for a couple of months. They gave me an evaluation and then sent me to Bronx Children's Psychiatric Center. I stayed there for four or five months, then I got moved to Children's Village, a residential treatment facility outside of New York City.

I got into major issues at Children's Village, and they sent me upstate to another facility. I had a hard time there because I was hardheaded and never wanted to listen. As I got into my teens, I started to become more cooperative and eventually went home. But during the time I was home, I was messing up bad. I felt like I was just adapting to being back outside in the real world, but I got sent back upstate.

This time, I learned from my mistakes and did better because I knew the program. I went home again, but it felt like there was a force trying to stop me from doing good. I couldn't stay out of trouble.

Now I'm 16 and I'm locked up again, in Horizon Juvenile Center. I feel like I have learned a lot from all this and now I'm a better person than I was in the past. I know what's best for me and I'm changing my life around. This is the last time I'm going to be in confinement.

~~~~~~

A Jailhouse Education

By Anonymous

You can get a good education in jail, just not the best. The teachers are good at their jobs; we just need to participate. They say you can bring a horse to water but you can't make him drink.

That's the main problem in here. We make it difficult to get a good education in jail. We're so used to the street mentality that we bring it here with us. You have people who never went to school and don't find any interest in it now. Everybody is an obstacle to everyone else.

It's like crabs in a bucket: Nobody wants to see the next guy succeed while they're still "in the bucket." We keep the good man down so he won't look better than the rest of us. In the end, we all just look like an ignorant group of kids who deserve to be in jail.

Personally, I like learning as long as a topic is interesting. If I can relate to a lesson, I'll participate and give my thoughts or ask questions. And if a teacher is cool and not strict, kids will participate more. I know that when I'm in a class, I'd like everybody to have input, whatever the topic is. That way, I won't stick out like a goody-goody and be the target for those who want to pull me back into the "bucket."

It's my own fault I'm in here. When I did what I did, I knew what I was doing and what a big risk I was taking. Now I have to deal with the consequences. I have to deal with the people, the rules, and the school arrangement. But we all make mistakes and this is one that I'll learn from.

~~~~~~~~~~~~~~~~~~~~~~~~~~~

From Foster Care to Detention

By Anonymous

I didn't ask for any of this to happen. I didn't want to grow up going through foster homes and juvenile centers. I didn't want to disappoint my mom and stepfather. I wanted to do good and be something in life.

I guess that all changed five years ago. At the age of 10 I got placed in a foster home. I recently returned home to live with my own family again, but when I was in care I went through more foster homes than I can count.

Growing up in foster care is never easy. I lived anywhere I got put—the Bronx, Queens, Harlem. At first, it was kind of scary to live with complete strangers, but after a while you get used to it. The different faces, races, food, schools, friends, you name it. I learned not to get comfortable anywhere.

Before, I'd been a good kid for the most part. But being in foster care brought out a part of me that I didn't know was there. The I-just-didn't-give-a-f--- part. As I reached my teens I began to smoke, fight, have sex, and do crimes.

Every time the caseworker who dealt with my family situation said, "You're going home soon," and then it didn't actually happen, I started to care less and less and get worse and worse. I was on the road to destruction: getting arrested, stealing, fighting, all kinds of stuff. I knew it would catch up to me sooner or later, and it sure did.

I admit that I did stupid stuff and that's why I'm here. Although, now that I'm locked up, I'm motivated to do better. This isn't a place I would like to spend my life in, and I know it gets much wilder than this in adult prisons.

When I get out, I want to stay out and do better. So while I'm here, this is practice for how to behave on the outside. When I get out I plan to finish high school, go to college, and become a journalist or a lawyer.

Rosa Perin

A Wake-Up Call

By Juanita Raymond

One night last year, Josue A., 17, was walking through a park with two friends and his 12-year-old brother. Josue said he was walking along without looking back to see what was going on. But all of a sudden when he turned back, he saw his brother and two friends robbing a man.

Josue felt shocked, he said later. He thought, "Why you gonna take something when you got money in your pocket?"

Moments later he heard a siren screaming toward them. He got so confused that he didn't know what to do. First he decided to run, but he felt like he couldn't, so he just stood there. With cop cars speeding toward them, "I felt like it was busted any way they tried to put it," he said. His friends ran, but Josue stopped and waited for the cops.

"I figured I could get away with it if I told them the true

story. But I was involved and should have looked out, is the way they saw it," he told me in a very low voice. Besides, a witness fingered all of them.

Josue was sent to jail. After three days, he was sent to criminal court, and he pleaded guilty, at the suggestion of his lawyer. He was sent to Riker's Island jail in New York City, for one month.

Josue hated the time he spent in jail, but in some ways, he said he's glad he got arrested. "It gave me a chance to look at who I am and what I can do in life. It gave me second thoughts," he said. He started feeling very disappointed in himself and felt that he had let his family down in so many ways. He had been considered very trustworthy in the family. Now he had lost that trust.

When Josue was in jail, seeing his family just made him want to go home, so he told his family they shouldn't come and visit him. But they said they were going to make him suffer like he'd made the family suffer.

"I was like, how did I make you suffer? I didn't get it," Josue said. "But when my aunt came, I was heartbroke. Her face was like she wanted to break down crying. She was like, 'You coming home next week?' I said yes, but I knew I wasn't going home."

In jail, Josue started regretting the things he did before, like selling his video games to get high and selling drugs. Josue had started smoking weed when he was 13 years old, when he was at his 15-year-old uncle's house.

His uncle said, "Try this." Josue tried the weed and he liked it. "It was like a friend to me then, it released my stress," he said. "Everything has consequences bad or good, but that's how I had to find it out myself."

At Riker's, days felt like weeks and weeks felt like years. Josue felt like he'd made mistakes in his life, but he also felt he wasn't the type who belonged in jail.

"Looking at those kids, I figured that wasn't me. But I wasn't no punk being quiet, I showed no fear even though I was scared out of my ass," he said. "When I was crying, I couldn't show it. They would jump on me."

Life in jail was very strict. He couldn't watch his favorite TV shows in the dayroom, he had to eat when everybody was eating, and the food—when I asked about the food, he said "tsss," shook his head and put his head down on the table. "I didn't even trust my food. I'd be looking at it, poking it with my fork. It was nasty," he said.

Josue started going for his GED in jail, but he wasn't learning much. "Teachers were scared, not really trying to teach," he said. "I liked to go to the computer room, use the Internet. But there was only one computer with the Internet and there was a fight over it and they closed the computer room."

Finally his lawyer found a program for him that helps kids adjust after being in jail, and he was released on probation. When he came out of jail, he saw how his family didn't trust him anymore. "That's when they started locking down on me. I felt like I was a cat and they was pitbulls chasing me," he said.

For most of the six months of the program, Josue stayed off drugs. He went on trips and learned how to be a peer educator. But near the end of the program, he started getting high again.

He was so happy to be on the street, he said, and "my body started urging for drugs again." One day a friend of Josue's said, "Take a pull," and Josue figured that one pull wouldn't hurt. Soon he was "seeing mad spots."

A parole officer noticed the way he was acting and told Josue that he would send him back to jail if he didn't stop smoking. But Josue said he "lost control" of his thinking, kept smoking weed, and ended up being sent to Phoenix House, a rehab center in upstate New York.

At Phoenix House, Josue felt very uncomfortable. It was like a prison to him, and they had people coming in from jail who made Josue nervous. He said he had to watch what he did and who he hung out with. But at Phoenix House, he finally stopped smoking weed.

Even though going to jail and rehab was difficult for him and his family, Josue said he's glad they kept him there because it woke him up to reality. When he came back from Phoenix House, he joined the Fortune Society, a support agency for people who have been in jail.

Now he's preparing for his GED in classes at the Fortune Society and he is learning how to become an HIV peer educator, who teaches people how to reduce their chance of getting infected. Josue is also working on his reading and writing. He said he knows now that he can work up to his goals—to graduate from school and find a good job. Josue said he thought he could never change his ways, and at first, he used to blame people for his mistakes.

> *Before, I thought that good things can't ever happen to me. I thought, 'there's no way out.' Now I know the way out.*

"I looked out at the whole city of New York and thought, 'This is all your fault,'" he said with his head down. "Before, I thought that good things can't ever happen to me. I'm living in the projects and it can't happen. I thought, there's no way out. Now I know the way out. My goals, I'm urging for them now."

Even so, it's hard for Josue to live this new life. His mother still doesn't trust him. "I come home late and she thinks the worst," he said. "I'm like, nah, I was at my girlfriend's house playing games, and she won't believe me." Josue said she feels better when he comes home with good reports from his parole officer.

He also doesn't get along with his old friends or his younger brother, who was part of the robbery but didn't get charged. Josue said his brother hasn't changed at all.

"When I'm with him in the house it's OK, but when we go outside, I go my separate way," he said. "My brother stays in the same spot. He figures he can get away with stuff. Some time he's gonna see."

And with his old friends, it's hello and goodbye. "Now people see all the changes and the positive stuff, and I feel discriminated against in my neighborhood," he said. "It takes a minute to put a bottle in the trash, but my old friends, they look at me like, 'Why don't you just throw that on the floor?' "

Now Josue hangs out with friends he met at Fortune, who have similar goals to him.

"I'd rather hang out with people here than the people on my block," Josue said. "It gives me a reason to do good stuff."

Juanita was 17 when she wrote this story.
She graduated from high school and went to college.

WRITE A LETTER!

PROBLEM

IDEAS

CHANGE

Froylan Garcia

Shocked into Action

By Olivia Rosenthal

When I was 14, a close family friend told me about a boy around my age who had been charged with breaking and entering and stealing an iPod. This boy was barely a teenager, but was facing time in an adult prison.

Our family friend was mentoring this boy and believed he had been framed by another teen. But what really shocked me was how over-the-top this punishment seemed, even if he was guilty. How could a boy who could have been my own classmate be sentenced to an adult prison for a nonviolent crime?

Although I've always had a keen interest in politics and social justice issues, I didn't know much about the juvenile justice system. The story sparked my desire to understand how the system worked. I began researching, reading reports, and talking to people who worked at an alternative-to-incarceration program near my apartment.

The more I learned, the more confused I became. For one thing, it quickly became clear that New York was spending millions annually to keep juvenile prisons open, despite numerous reports that said these facilities didn't get kids to stop committing crimes.

I also discovered there weren't many good programs to help released youth avoid getting into trouble again. As a result, in some years the rate of recidivism (that's the percentage of prisoners who are re-arrested within a short period after release) topped 60%. (The numbers are even higher for 16-to-18-year-olds, who are considered adults in the system). With these rates so high, it became clear to me that lives all around me were being wasted and destroyed in prison.

In a stroke of luck, I was already volunteering at New York State Senator Eric Schneiderman's office. I took the opportunity to start researching laws that could improve the state's juvenile justice system.

My research showed me that this issue was receiving too little public attention. This became clear as I explained my research to family and friends, many of whom were extremely politically active, and they were surprised by my findings. I felt a responsibility to inform others about what was happening to my peers.

I decided to create a pamphlet aimed at fellow teenagers. In it I corrected common misunderstandings about the juvenile justice system. For example, I pointed out that in spite of the perception that juvenile crime is high in New York state, it's actually dropped in recent years. Despite this drop, however, the state continues to operate juvenile prisons with many empty beds. I also used the pamphlet to advocate for alternative-to-incarceration programs that provide things like counseling and job training.

Once my pamphlet was completed, I tried to find a way to distribute it at public schools or at nonprofit organizations. I realized that if the statistics I'd uncovered shocked me, they would likely shock my peers across the state. I hoped that by informing others, I'd inspire them to advocate for change.

I e-mailed hundreds of organizations, politicians, lawyers, and others I felt were in a position to help the cause. At first, I was reluctant to attach my pamphlet to the e-mails. I was only 16 and I worried that these professionals, who'd spent so much more time working on this issue than I had, would dismiss or poke holes in my research.

However, it turned out just the opposite way. After countless e-mails went unanswered, I decided to go ahead and send people my pamphlet. Once I had a legitimate project to show them, I started to get some responses. Before I knew it, I was talking with administrators at New Visions public schools about writing my own lesson plan to teach their students about the juvenile justice system, and speaking with a congressman from Virginia about how to adapt federal legislation to my own neighborhood.

I hoped that by informing others, I'd inspire them to advocate for change.

With the support of Senator Schneiderman, I also began working on a state version of the federal Youth Promise Act, an effort to support youth and prevent juvenile crime. Although it's a lengthy project and I'm still working on completing the bill, I'm hopeful it'll be ready to be submitted to legislative committees by early next year. I'm still somewhat in shock that from a few years' work, I might actually be able to impact state policy.

My experience with youth justice has taught me that you are never too young to effect change. If you trust your own opinions and then get the facts to back those opinions up and set goals, you'll find that there are ways to impact the world around you. Now when I walk into the juvenile crime prevention program in my neighborhood and hear stories of arrests, I can actually understand the teens' dilemmas and sometimes even offer possible solutions.

If you see a problem in the world beyond your school walls

you can—with hard work, dedication, and I guess you could say pushiness—make a difference. Ultimately, I think most of my work has come from the belief that other teenagers will be moved to join the struggle for change, if only they're properly informed about what's really happening.

So whether you are interested in youth justice or another issue, I urge you to not assume that adults will take care of it. Take matters into your own hands, because something this important is everybody's business.

Olivia was 17 when she wrote this story.

Teens:
How to Get More Out of This Book

Self-help: The teens who wrote the stories in this book did so because they hope that telling their stories will help readers who are facing similar challenges. They want you to know that you are not alone, and that taking specific steps can help you manage or overcome very difficult situations. They've done their best to be clear about the actions that worked for them so you can see if they'll work for you.

Writing: You can also use the book to improve your writing skills. Each teen in this book wrote 5-10 drafts of his or her story before it was published. If you read the stories closely you'll see that the teens work to include a beginning, a middle, and an end, and good scenes, description, dialogue, and anecdotes (little stories). To improve your writing, take a look at how these writers construct their stories. Try some of their techniques in your own writing.

Reading: Finally, you'll notice that we include the first chapter from a Bluford Series novel in this book, alongside the true stories by teens. We hope you'll like it enough to continue reading. The more you read, the more you'll strengthen your reading skills. Teens at Youth Communication like the Bluford novels because they explore themes similar to those in their own stories. Your school may already have the Bluford books. If not, you can order them online for only $1.

How to Use This Book in Staff Training

Staff say that reading these stories gives them greater insight into what teens are thinking and feeling, and new strategies for working with them. You can help the staff you work with by using these stories as case studies.

Select one story to read in the group, and ask staff to identify and discuss the main issue facing the teen. There may be disagreement about this, based on the background and experience of staff. That is fine. One point of the exercise is that teens have complex lives and needs. Adults can probably be more effective if they don't focus too narrowly and can see several dimensions of their clients.

Ask staff: What issues or feelings does the story provoke in them? What kind of help do they think the teen wants? What interventions are likely to be most promising? Least effective? Why? How would you build trust with the teen writer? How have other adults failed the teen, and how might that affect his or her willingness to accept help? What other resources would be helpful to this teen, such as peer support, a mentor, counseling, family therapy, etc?

Discussion Guide

Teachers and Staff:
How to Use This Book in Groups

When working with teens individually or in groups, you can use these stories to help young people face difficult issues in a way that feels safe to them. That's because talking about the issues in the stories usually feels safer to teens than talking about those same issues in their own lives. Addressing issues through the stories allows for some personal distance; they hit close to home, but not too close. Talking about them opens up a safe place for reflection. As teens gain confidence talking about the issues in the stories, they usually become more comfortable talking about those issues in their own lives.

Below are general questions to guide your discussion. In most cases you can read a story and conduct a discussion in one 45-minute session. Teens are usually happy to read the stories aloud, with each teen reading a paragraph or two. (Allow teens to pass if they don't want to read.) It takes 10-15 minutes to read a story straight through. However, it is often more effective to let workshop participants make comments and discuss the story as you go along. The workshop leader may even want to annotate her copy of the story beforehand with key questions.

If teens read the story ahead of time or silently, it's good to break the ice with a few questions that get everyone on the same page: Who is the main character? How old is she? What happened to her? How did she respond? Another good starting question is: "What stood out for you in the story?" Go around the room and let each person briefly mention one thing.

Then move on to open-ended questions, which encourage participants to think more deeply about what the writers were feeling, the choices they faced, and the actions they took. There are no right or wrong answers to the open-ended questions.

About
Youth Communication

Youth Communication, founded in 1980, is a nonprofit youth development program located in New York City whose mission is to teach writing, journalism, and leadership skills. The teenagers we train become writers for our websites and books and for two print magazines: *New Youth Connections*, a general-interest youth magazine, and *Represent*, a magazine by and for young people in foster care.

Each year, up to 100 young people participate in Youth Communication's after school and summer journalism workshops, where they work under the direction of full-time professional editors. Most are African-American, Latino, or Asian, and many are recent immigrants. The opportunity to reach their peers with accurate portrayals of their lives and important self-help information motivates the young writers to create powerful stories.

Our goal is to run a strong youth development program in which teens produce high quality stories that inform and inspire their peers. Doing so requires us to be sensitive to the complicated lives and emotions of the teen participants while also providing an intellectually rigorous experience. We achieve that goal in the writing/teaching/editing relationship, which is the core of our program.

Our teaching and editorial process begins with discussions

between adult editors and the teen staff. In those meetings, the teens and the editors work together to identify the most important issues in the teens' lives and to figure out how those issues can be turned into stories that will resonate with teen readers.

Once story topics are chosen, students begin the process of crafting their stories. For a personal story, that means revisiting events in one's past to understand their significance for the future. For a commentary, it means developing a logical and persuasive point of view. For a reported story, it means gathering information through research and interviews. Students look inward and outward as they try to make sense of their experiences and the world around them and find the points of intersection between personal and social concerns. That process can take a few weeks or a few months. Stories frequently go through 10 or more drafts as students work under the guidance of their editors, the way any professional writer does.

Many of the students who walk through our doors have uneven skills, as a result of poor education, living under extremely stressful conditions, or coming from homes where English is a second language. Yet, to complete their stories, students must successfully perform a wide range of activities, including writing and rewriting, reading, discussion, reflection, research, interviewing, and typing. They must work as members of a team and they must accept individual responsibility. They learn to provide constructive criticism, and to accept it. They engage in explorations of truthfulness, fairness, and accuracy. They meet deadlines. They must develop the audacity to believe that they have something important to say and the humility to recognize that saying it well is not a process of instant gratification. Rather, it usually requires a long, hard struggle through many discussions and much rewriting.

It would be impossible to teach these skills and dispositions as separate, disconnected topics, like grammar, ethics, or assertiveness. However, we find that students make rapid progress when they are learning skills in the context of an inquiry that is personally significant to them and that will benefit their peers.

When teens publish their stories—in *New Youth Connections* and *Represent*, on the Web, and in other publications—they reach tens of thousands of teen and adult readers. Teachers, counselors, social workers, and other adults circulate the stories to young people in their classes and out-of-school youth programs. Adults tell us that teens in their programs—including many who are ordinarily resistant to reading—clamor for the stories. Teen readers report that the stories give them information they can't get anywhere else, and inspire them to reflect on their lives and open lines of communication with adults.

Writers usually participate in our program for one semester, though some stay much longer. Years later, many of them report that working here was a turning point in their lives—that it helped them acquire the confidence and skills that they needed for success in college and careers. Scores of our graduates have overcome tremendous obstacles to become journalists, writers, and novelists. They include National Book Award finalist and MacArthur Fellowship winner Edwidge Danticat, novelist Ernesto Quiñonez, writer Veronica Chambers, and *New York Times* reporter Rachel Swarns. Hundreds more are working in law, business, and other careers. Many are teachers, principals, and youth workers, and several have started nonprofit youth programs themselves and work as mentors—helping another generation of young people develop their skills and find their voices.

Youth Communication is a nonprofit educational corporation. Contributions are gratefully accepted and are tax deductible to the fullest extent of the law.

To make a contribution, or for information about our publications and programs, including our catalog of over 100 books and curricula for hard-to-reach teens, see www.youthcomm.org.

About the Editors

Laura Longhine is the editorial director at Youth Communication, where she oversees editorial work on the organization's books, websites, and magazines. She edited *Represent,* Youth Communication's magazine by and for teens in foster care, for three years.

Prior to joining Youth Communication, Longhine was as a staff writer at the *Free Times,* an alt-weekly in South Carolina, and a freelance reporter for various publications. Her stories have been published in *The New York Times, Legal Affairs,* newyorkmetro.com, and *Child Welfare Watch.* She has a bachelor's in English from Tufts University and a master's in journalism from Columbia University.

Longhine is the editor of several other Youth Communication books, including *Watching My Parents Disappear: Teens Write About Living with Drug Addiction* and *Analyze This! A Teen Guide to Therapy and Getting Help.*

Keith Hefner co-founded Youth Communication in 1980 and has directed it ever since. He is the recipient of the Luther P. Jackson Education Award from the New York Association of Black Journalists and a MacArthur Fellowship. He was also a Revson Fellow at Columbia University.

HELP YOUNG MEN SUCCEED

More Helpful Books
From Youth Communication

The Struggle to Be Strong: True Stories by Teens About Overcoming Tough Times. Foreword by Veronica Chambers. Help young people identify and build on their own strengths with 30 personal stories about resiliency. (Free Spirit)

Starting With "I": Personal Stories by Teenagers. "Who am I and who do I want to become?" Thirty-five stories examine this question through the lens of race, ethnicity, gender, sexuality, family, and more. Increase this book's value with the free Teacher's Guide, available from youthcomm.org. (Youth Communication)

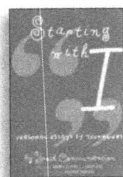

Real Men. Empower young men of color to break through limiting stereotypes and make positive choices about the kind of men they want to be. The complete program includes an anthology, leaders guide with 36 lessons, and a DVD. (Youth Communication)

The Courage to Be Yourself: True Stories by Teens About Cliques, Conflicts, and Overcoming Peer Pressure. In 26 first-person stories, teens write about their lives with searing honesty. These stories will inspire young readers to reflect on their own lives, work through their problems, and help them discover who they really are. (Free Spirit)

Out With It: Gay and Straight Teens Write About Homosexuality. Break stereotypes and provide support with this unflinching look at gay life from a teen's perspective. With a focus on urban youth, this book also includes several heterosexual teens' transformative experiences with gay peers. (Youth Communication)

Things Get Hectic: Teens Write About the Violence That Surrounds Them. Violence is commonplace in many teens' lives, be it bullying, gangs, dating, or family relationships. Hear the experiences of victims, perpetrators, and witnesses through more than 50 real-world stories. (Youth Communication)

From Dropout to Achiever: Teens Write About School. Help teens overcome the challenges of graduating, which may involve overcoming family problems, bouncing back from a bad semester, or even dropping out for a time. These teens show how they achieve academic success. (Youth Communication)

My Secret Addiction: Teens Write About Cutting. These true accounts of cutting, or self-mutilation, offer a window into the personal and family situations that lead to this secret habit, and show how teens can get the help they need. (Youth Communication)

Sticks and Stones: Teens Write About Bullying. Shed light on bullying, with stories told from the perspectives of the bully, the victim, and the witness. These stories show why bullying occurs, the harm it causes, and how it might be prevented. (Youth Communication)

Boys to Men: Teens Write About Becoming a Man. The young men in this book write about confronting the challenges of growing up. Their honesty and courage make them role models for teens who are bombarded with contradictory messages about what it means to be a man. (Youth Communication)

Through Thick and Thin: Teens Write About Obesity, Eating Disorders, and Self Image. Help teens who struggle with obesity, eating disorders, and body image issues. These stories show the pressures teens face when they are confronted by unrealistic standards for physical appearance, and how emotions can affect the way we eat. (Youth Communication)

To order these and other books, go to:
www.youthcomm.org
or call 212-279-0708 x115

www.ingramcontent.com/pod-product-compliance
Lightning Source LLC
Chambersburg PA
CBHW071228290326
41931CB00037B/2454